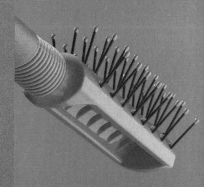

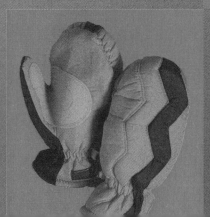

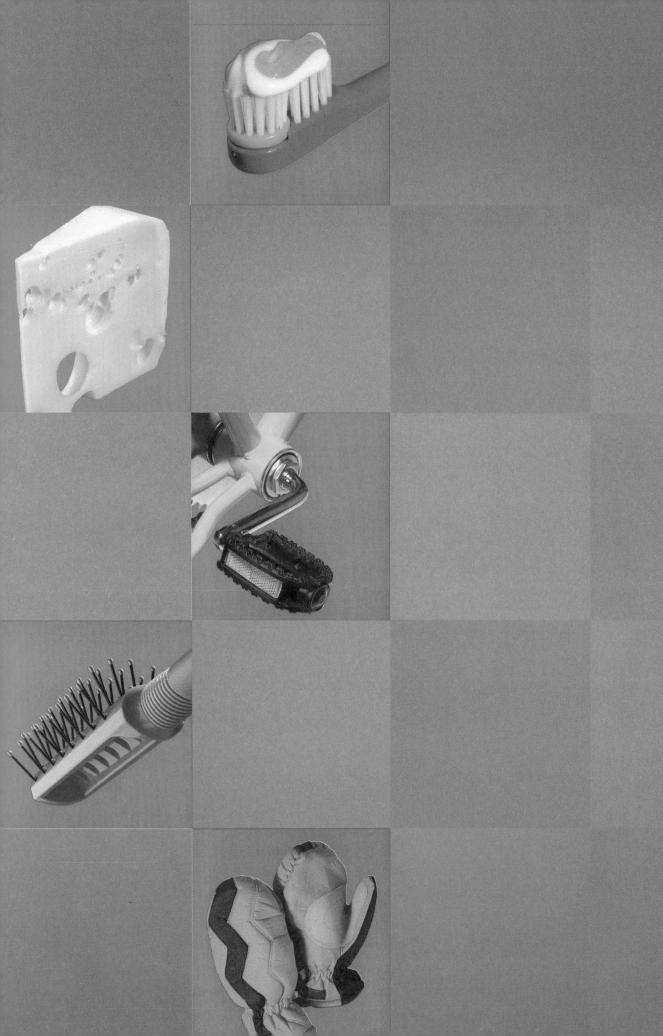

YOUR Health

Harcourt

Orlando • Austin • Chicago • New York • Toronto • London • San Diego

Visit *The Learning Site!*
www.harcourtschool.com

CONSULTING AUTHORS

Charlie Gibbons, Ed.D.
Associate Professor
Alabama State University
Health, Physical Education and Dance Department
Montgomery, Alabama
School Age Coordinator
Maxwell Air Force Base, Alabama

Jan Marie Ozias, Ph.D., R.N.
Director, Texas Diabetes Council
Consultant, School Health Programs
Austin, Texas

Carl Anthony Stockton, Ph.D.
Professor of Health Education and Department Chair
Department of Health, Physical Education, and Recreation
The University of North Carolina at Wilmington
Wilmington, North Carolina

Printed in the United States of America

ISBN 0-15-334302-8

1 2 3 4 5 6 7 8 9 10 048 10 09 08 07 06 05 04 03 02

Contents

Emotional,
Intellectual,
and Social
Health

Chapter 5 — Preventing Disease 120

Disease Prevention and Control

Chapter 6 — Medicine and Other Drugs . . 146

Drug Use Prevention

Chapter 9   Health in the Community .. 220

Community and Environmental Health

Health Handbook 244

Understanding Life Skills

Having good health isn't just knowing the facts. It's also thinking critically about those facts and knowing how to use them every day. The Life Skills in *Your Health* can help you do just that.

Setting Goals for Self Improvement

In soccer or ice hockey, scoring a goal is something that a team wants to do to win the game. In life, you set goals for things you want to do to improve yourself. Planning and checking your progress makes it easy. You feel better about yourself because you know you are getting closer to your goals.

▶ **Roosevelt knows that it is important to his health to exercise. How can he set a goal to exercise more during the week?**

Steps for Setting Goals

1. Set a goal.

2. List and plan steps to meet that goal.

3. Check your progress toward the goal.

4. Evaluate the goal.

Making Decisions

Decisions that affect your health are important. For important decisions, you should think carefully about all the choices and the possible results, then decide. Following the steps shown below will help you make wise decisions. Making wise decisions will help to keep you healthy.

Think about your choices!

◄ Trisha is at her friend's house after school and becomes thirsty. Her friend offers Trisha a sip of her drink. How can Trisha make the best decision?

Steps for Making Decisions

1. Find out about the choices you could make.

2. Imagine the possible result of each choice.

3. Make what seems to be the best choice.

4. Think about the result of your choice.

🍎 Managing Stress

"I'm so stressed!" Maybe you or a parent said that today. Stress is tension in your body or your mind. Maybe you feel stress because of a class report, a quiz, or a doctor's appointment. Some stress is a normal part of life. You even need a little stress to stay healthy. But, it's important not to let stress harm your health.

▶ **Tomorrow is the first day Camille is going to a new school. She is nervous about making new friends. How can she manage her stress and relax?**

Steps for Managing Stress

1. Know what stress feels like and what causes it.

2. When you feel stress, think about ways to handle it.

3. Focus on one step at a time.

4. Learn ways to reduce and release tension.

Refusing

Sometimes people can try to make you do things you really don't want to do. Knowing how to refuse, or say *no*, to things that are unsafe or risky can keep you healthy. This is also an important reason for learning more about your health. Knowing how a bad choice—such as using alcohol, tobacco, or other drugs—will affect you makes it easier to say *no* firmly.

▶ **Todd is at a sleep-over with his friends. Some of them want to watch a movie that he knows his family wouldn't want to him to see. How can Todd refuse watching the movie?**

How to Refuse

1. Say **no** and say why not.

2. State your reasons for saying **no**.

3. Suggest something else to do.

4. Repeat **no**; walk away.

Communicating

Communicating is another word for "sharing information."
You have ideas, needs, and feelings. To meet your needs,
you often need to communicate with other people. You also
need to listen to people and understand their needs and
feelings.

◀ Ever since Bradley's
little sister was born, he
feels he is getting less
attention from his
parents. Yet, he loves
his new sister. How can
he communicate his
feelings to his parents?

How to Communicate

1. Understand your audience.
2. Give a clear message.
3. Listen.
4. Gather feedback.

Resolving Conflicts

Conflict, or disagreement, is a normal part of life. Disagreeing with a classmate about how to finish a project is a conflict. Bigger conflicts may lead to hurt feelings or even violence. A fight or an argument is a poor way to deal with a conflict. If you communicate well, you often can find a peaceful way to resolve, or end, a conflict. You may even find that communicating well leads to a solution that is better for everyone.

▶ **Yuriko's older brother took a CD from her room. He says that the CD is his, and that Yuriko took it from him. How can they resolve this conflict?**

Steps for Resolving Conflicts

1. **Use I-messages to tell how you feel.**

2. **Listen to each other.**

3. **Think of the other person's point of view.**

4. **Decide what to do and do it.**

Being a Wise Health Consumer

Being a wise consumer means making good buying decisions. As you get older, you will have more responsibility for buying health products and services. You need to learn how advertisements can mislead you. You also need to learn how to get valid, or correct, health information.

 ## Making Buying Decisions

Advertising can help you make buying decisions. However, advertisements shouldn't be the only information you use. Using product information wisely helps you to get the most value for your money.

▲ Which of these backpacks would you choose to buy? Why?

Steps for Making Buying Decisions

1. Decide whether the item is something you need, want, or don't really need at all.

2. Compare several brands of the same item.

3. Choose the least expensive item that meets your needs.

4. Think about the result of your purchase decision.

 # Analyzing Advertising and Media Messages

Advertising is everywhere, even places you may not notice. Ads can give you good information about a product. They also can mislead you. Be aware of these tricks to get you to buy:

PUT DOWN

TRICK The ad says another product is bad.

TIP Maybe the other brand isn't that bad. Compare the products for yourself.

IDEAL PEOPLE

TRICK Everyone in the ad looks pretty and happy.

TIP The product doesn't make people pretty or happy. Find out what it really does.

BE COOL

TRICK People who use the product become more popular.

TIP A product can't make someone more popular.

JOIN THE CROWD

TRICK It seems like everyone is using this product and you're left out.

TIP Most people probably aren't using the product. It's wise to buy only things that you need.

STAR POWER

TRICK Your favorite sports or music star tells you to buy a product.

TIP The star can't know that the product is right for you. Find out if it really meets your needs.

How to Analyze Advertising and Media Messages

1. **Find out who made the message and why.**

2. **Watch for tricks to make you notice or agree with the message.**

3. **Notice the values and points of view shown.**

4. **Learn whether anything is left out.**

Accessing Valid Health Information

It's important to know the facts about your health. However, not everything you read or see is the truth. You should make sure health information is reliable, or trustworthy. The best source of health information is health professionals, such as nurses, doctors, and pharmacists. For other sources, especially the Internet, you should think about the source of the information. Also, check to see if other sources agree.

Sources That Are Probably Reliable

- College and university websites
- Science and health journals
- Major national newspapers
- National health magazines
- National health organizations, such as the American Heart Association
- Government organizations, such as the Centers for Disease Control and Prevention

Access Valid Health Information

1. Find out who is responsible for the information. Notice whether they are selling something.

2. Decide if the information is reasonable.

3. Check the information against other reliable sources. Keep a questioning attitude.

4. Discuss the information with a trusted adult or a health professional such as a nurse, doctor, or pharmacist.

You will learn and practice these important life skills as you use _Your Health_.

The Amazing Human Body

Getting enough rest, staying active, and eating right are important steps to a healthful life.

Sense Organs

Eye

Your eyes are protected by the bones in your skull, nose, and cheeks. Your eyelids protect your eyes automatically from dust, tiny flying objects, and sudden bright lights.

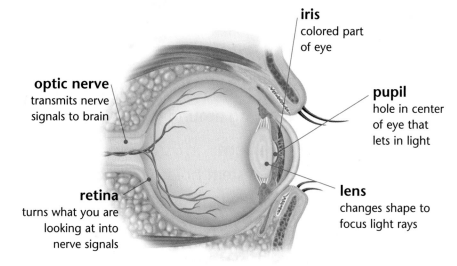

iris
colored part of eye

optic nerve
transmits nerve signals to brain

pupil
hole in center of eye that lets in light

retina
turns what you are looking at into nerve signals

lens
changes shape to focus light rays

Ear

Earwax is made inside your ears to help keep them clean. Dust, dirt, and germs stick to the earwax instead of going farther into your ear. When you move your mouth by chewing and talking, old wax works its way to your outer ear.

Outer ear   **Middle ear**   **Inner ear**

eardrum
moves back and forth when hit by sound waves

ear canal
connects outer ear to middle ear

Caring for Your Eyes and Ears

- Have your eyesight (vision) checked every year.

- Wear safety glasses when participating in activities that can be dangerous to the eyes, such as sports and mowing grass.

- Wash in, around, and behind your outer ear. Do not try to clean your ear canal with cotton-tip sticks or other objects.

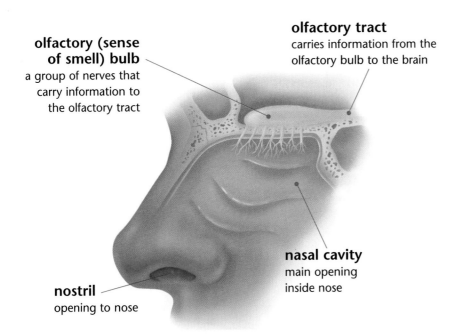

olfactory (sense of smell) bulb
a group of nerves that carry information to the olfactory tract

olfactory tract
carries information from the olfactory bulb to the brain

nasal cavity
main opening inside nose

nostril
opening to nose

Nose

The inside of your nose is lined with tiny blood vessels. When something hits you in the nose, these blood vessels can break and you can have a nosebleed.

Tongue

Germs live on your tongue and in other parts of your mouth. Germs can harm your teeth and give you bad breath.

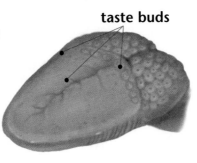

taste buds

Skin

Your skin protects your insides from the outside world. It keeps fluids you need inside your body and fluids you don't need, such as swimming pool water, outside your body.

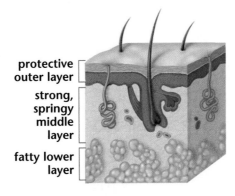

protective outer layer

strong, springy middle layer

fatty lower layer

Caring for Your Nose, Tongue, and Skin

- If you get a nosebleed, sit, lean forward slightly, and pinch just below the bridge of your nose for ten minutes. Breathe through your mouth.

- When you brush your teeth, brush your tongue too.

- Always wear sunscreen when you are in the sun.

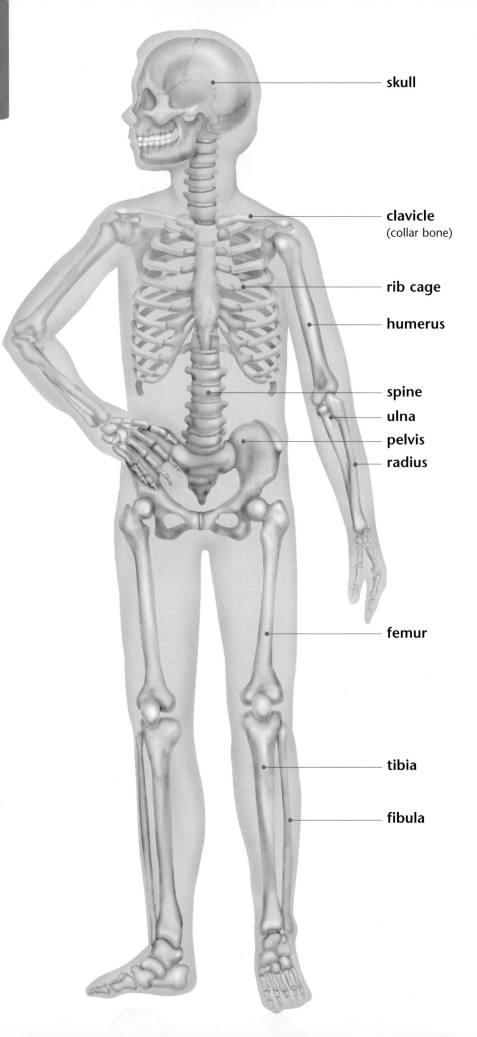

Each of your bones has a particular shape and size that allow it to do a certain job. You have bones that are tiny, long, wide, flat, and even curved. The job of some bones is to protect your body parts.

skull

clavicle
(collar bone)

rib cage

humerus

spine

ulna

pelvis

radius

femur

tibia

fibula

Bones that Protect

Rib Cage Your rib bones form a cage that protects your heart and lungs from all sides. Your ribs are springy. When something strikes you in the chest, your ribs push the object away instead of letting it hit your heart and lungs. Your ribs are connected to your breastbone (sternum) by springy material called cartilage. The springy connection lets your ribs move up and down. This happens when your rib cage gets bigger and smaller as you breathe in and out.

cartilage

rib

sternum

Skull The bones in your head are called your skull. Some of the bones in your skull protect your brain. The bones in your face are part of your skull too.

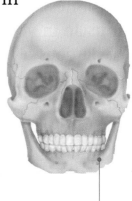

jaw

Caring for Your Skeletal System

- Calcium helps bones grow and makes them strong. Dairy products like milk, cheese, and yogurt contain calcium. Have 2–3 servings of dairy products every day.

- Exercise also makes your bones strong. When bones aren't used, they can become brittle and may break.

Activities

1. Look at the picture of the skeleton. Name a long bone. Name a short bone. Name a curved bone.

2. Put a tomato inside a wire cage. Gently throw a wad of paper at the cage. What happens? The cage protects the tomato in the same way your ribs protect your heart.

3. Measure around your rib cage with a string. How big is it when you breathe in? How big is it when you breathe out? Which measurement is greater?

Muscular System

ike your bones, each muscle in your body does a certain job. Muscles in your thumb help you hold things. Muscles in your neck help you turn your head. Muscles in your arms help you pull or lift objects.

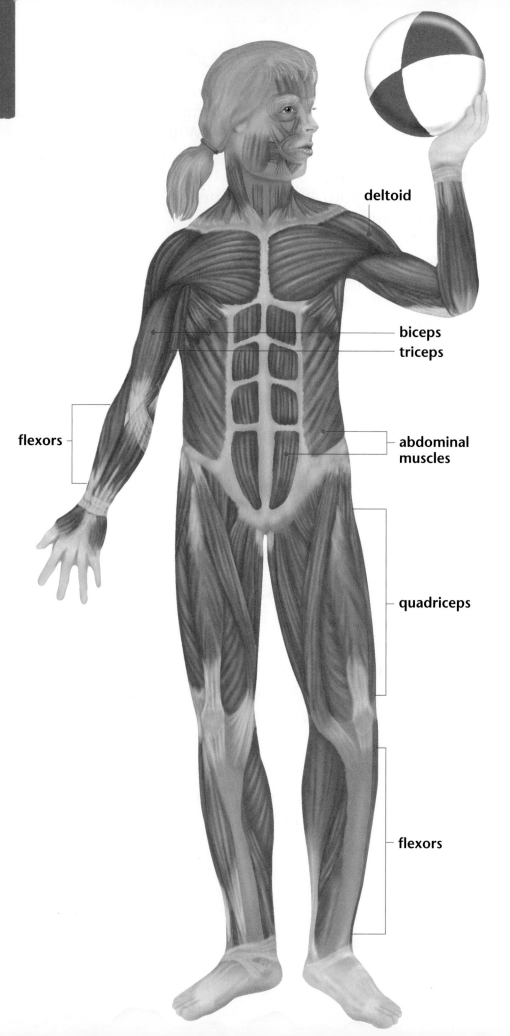

deltoid

biceps

triceps

flexors

abdominal muscles

quadriceps

flexors

How Muscles Move Your Body

Muscle Pairs Your arm can reach forward and pull back. Your hand can open and close. Muscles can only pull. Moving part of your body in more than one direction takes more than one muscle. It takes a pair of muscles for your arm to bend and straighten.

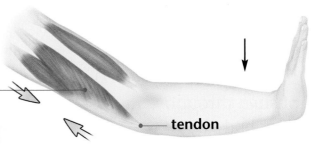

triceps contracts when you straighten your arm

tendon

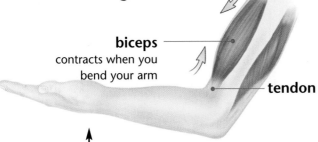

biceps contracts when you bend your arm

tendon

Tendons Tendons are strong strips of tough cord-like material. They connect your muscles to your bones. Your Achilles tendon is just above your heel. It connects your calf muscle to your heel bone. Your calf muscles and Achilles tendon allow you to stand on tiptoe.

Caring for Your Muscular System

- Exercise makes your muscles stronger.
- Stretching before you exercise makes muscles and tendons more flexible and less likely to get hurt.

Activities

1. Tie your shoe without using your thumb. What happens?

2. Pull up on a desk with one hand. With your other hand, feel which arm muscle is working. Now push on the desk. Which arm muscle is working?

3. Ask a friend to push down on your arms for one minute while you push up as hard as you can. When your friend lets go, what happens?

Digestive System

Food is broken down and pushed through your body by your digestive system. Your digestive system is a series of connected parts that starts with your mouth and ends with your large intestine.

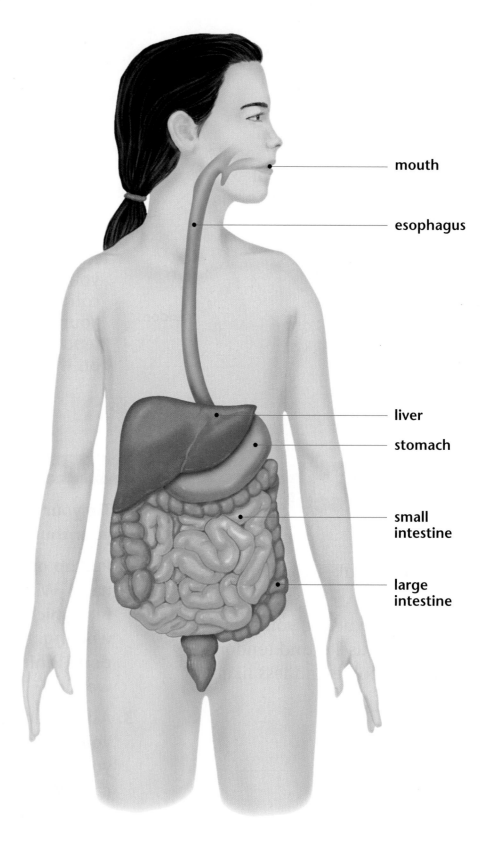

mouth

esophagus

liver

stomach

small intestine

large intestine

From Mouth to Stomach

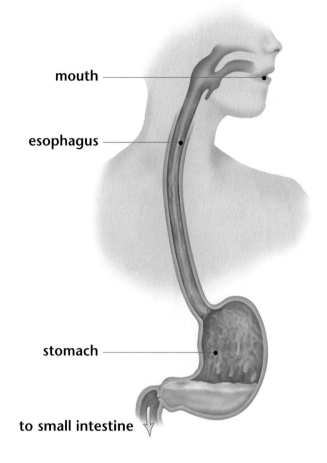

mouth

esophagus

stomach

to small intestine

Esophagus Your esophagus, or food tube, is a tube that connects your mouth to your stomach. After you swallow a bite of food, muscles in your esophagus push the food into your stomach.

Stomach Your stomach is filled with acid that helps dissolve food. The stomach walls are strong muscles that mix food with the acid. The stomach walls are protected from the acid by a thick layer of mucus. From your stomach, food moves to the small intestine and then to the large intestine.

Caring for Your Digestive System

- Chew everything you eat carefully. Well-chewed food is easier to digest.

- Do not overeat. Overeating can cause a stomachache.

Activities

1. Measure 25 feet (about 8 m) on the floor. This is how long your digestive system is.

2. Cut a narrow balloon so that it is open on both ends. Put a wad of paper in one end. Squeeze the outside of the balloon to push the paper through and out the other end. This is similar to how your esophagus pushes food to your stomach.

Circulatory System

Food and oxygen travel through your circulatory system to every cell in your body. Blood moves nutrients throughout your body, fights infection, and helps control your body temperature. Your blood is made up mostly of a watery liquid called plasma.

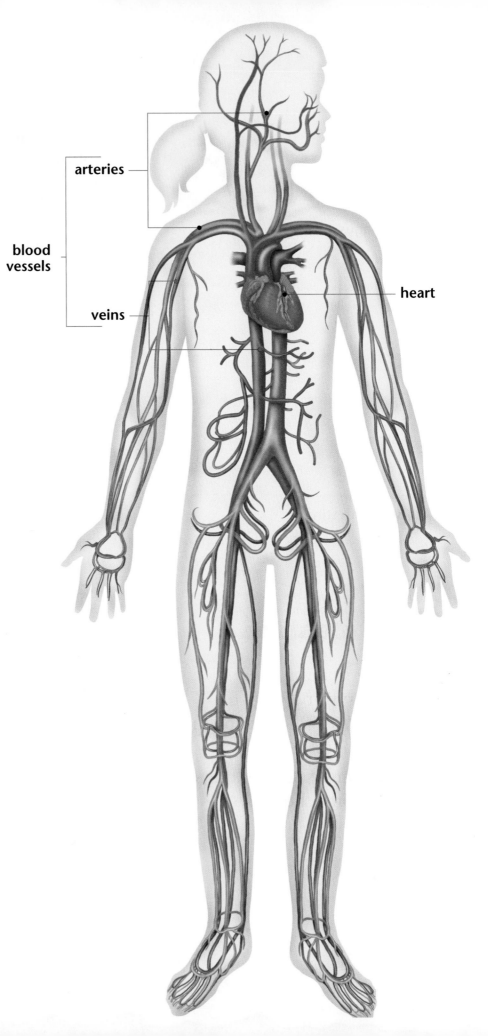

arteries

blood vessels

veins

heart

Blood Vessels

Arteries Arteries carry blood away from the heart. Blood in arteries is brighter red because it has come from the lungs and has lots of oxygen. Arteries bring oxygen and nutrients to all parts of the body.

Veins Veins carry blood to the heart. Veins have one-way valves that allow blood to move only toward the heart.

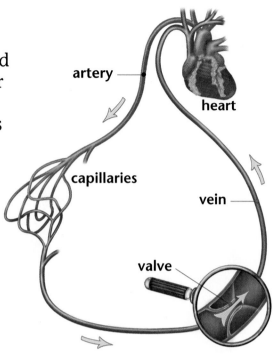

artery

heart

capillaries

vein

valve

Capillaries Capillaries are very small pathways for blood. When blood flows through capillaries, it gives oxygen and nutrients to the cells in your body. Blood also picks up carbon dioxide and other waste.

Caring for Your Circulatory System

- Never touch another person's blood.
- Eat a healthy, balanced diet throughout your life to keep excess fat from blocking the blood flowing through your arteries.
- Get regular exercise to keep your heart strong.

Activities

1. Take the bottom out of a paper cup. Bend the top together like a clamshell. Hold the cup and drop a marble through from the bottom. Now try to drop one into the top. The clamshell-shaped cup is like the one-way valve in a vein.

2. Find the blue lines under the skin on your wrist. These are veins. Press gently and stroke along the lines toward your elbow. Now stroke toward your hand. What do you see?

Respiratory System

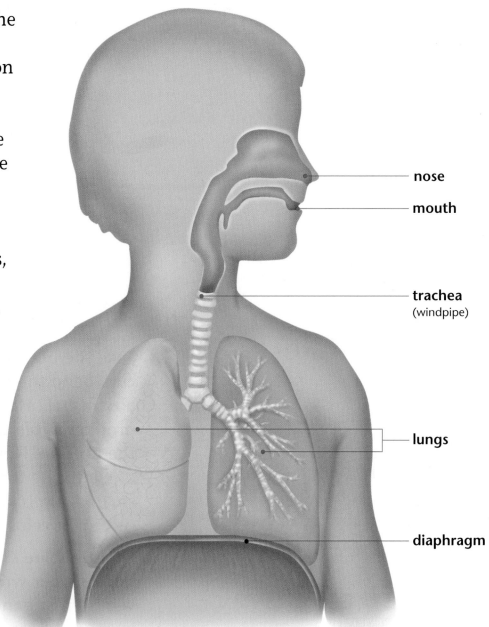

Your body uses its respiratory system to get oxygen from the air and get rid of excess carbon dioxide. Your respiratory system is made up of your nose and mouth, your trachea (windpipe), your two lungs, and your diaphragm—a dome-shaped muscle under your lungs.

nose

mouth

trachea
(windpipe)

lungs

diaphragm

Breathing

When you inhale, or breathe in, air enters your mouth and nose and goes into your trachea. Your trachea connects your nose and mouth to your lungs. Your trachea divides into two smaller tubes that go to your lungs. Your lungs fill with air. When you exhale, or breathe out, your diaphragm pushes upward. Air is forced up your trachea and out your mouth and nose.

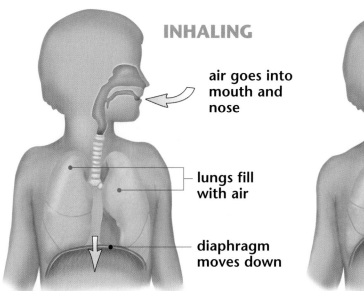

INHALING

air goes into mouth and nose

lungs fill with air

diaphragm moves down

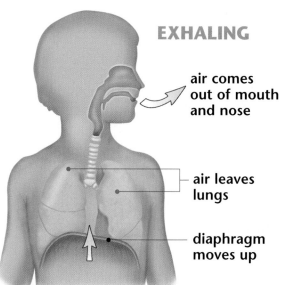

EXHALING

air comes out of mouth and nose

air leaves lungs

diaphragm moves up

Caring for Your Respiratory System

- Exercise. When you exercise your body, you exercise your respiratory system too. Your muscles use more oxygen, so you breathe faster and deeper.

- Get enough sleep to help your resistance to colds.

Activities

1. Sit in a chair and count how many breaths you take in 30 seconds. Then exercise for two minutes. When you stop, count how many breaths you take in 30 seconds. Do you breathe more while sitting or after exercise?

2. Put your hand on your bellybutton and take a deep breath in and out. How does your hand move?

Your nerves send information to your brain from various parts of your body and from the outside world. Your brain decides what to do with the information and sends instructions through your nerves back to your body parts.

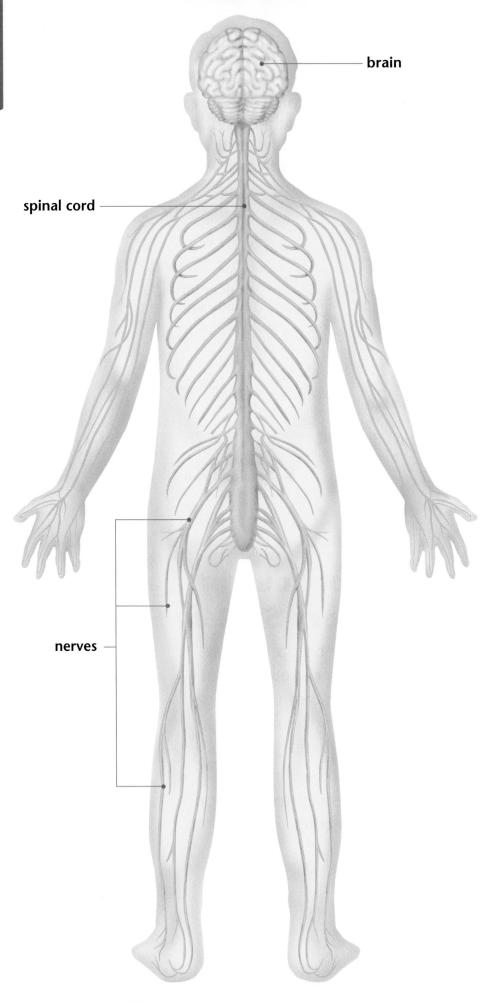

brain

spinal cord

nerves

Your Brain

Your brain is about two pounds of wrinkled, pinkish-gray material. It's protected by your skull and cushioned by a thin layer of liquid. The brain's main connection to the body is the spinal cord.

Different parts of the brain send signals to different parts of your body. For example, the part right behind your forehead tells your body how to move. The area near the base of your neck controls your breathing and heartbeat. If you are left-handed, the right half of your brain controls your handwriting.

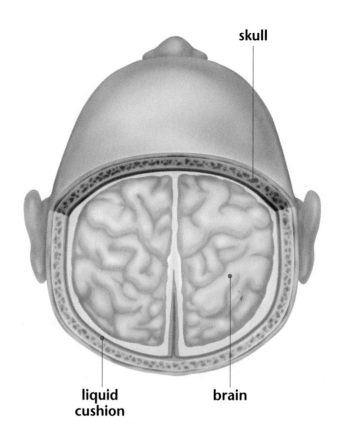

skull

liquid cushion

brain

Caring for Your Nervous System

- Many injuries to the brain are caused by car crashes. Wear your safety belt and sit in the backseat when you are in the car.

- Always wear a helmet when you ride your bike or scooter, skate, or use a skateboard.

Activities

1. Make a list of signals your nerves are sending to your brain right now. Also list instructions your brain is sending to your nerves.

2. Read a paragraph out of a book while the television is on. Do you know what the paragraph was about? Do you know what happened on television?

3. Write your name with your opposite hand ten times. Does your writing improve?

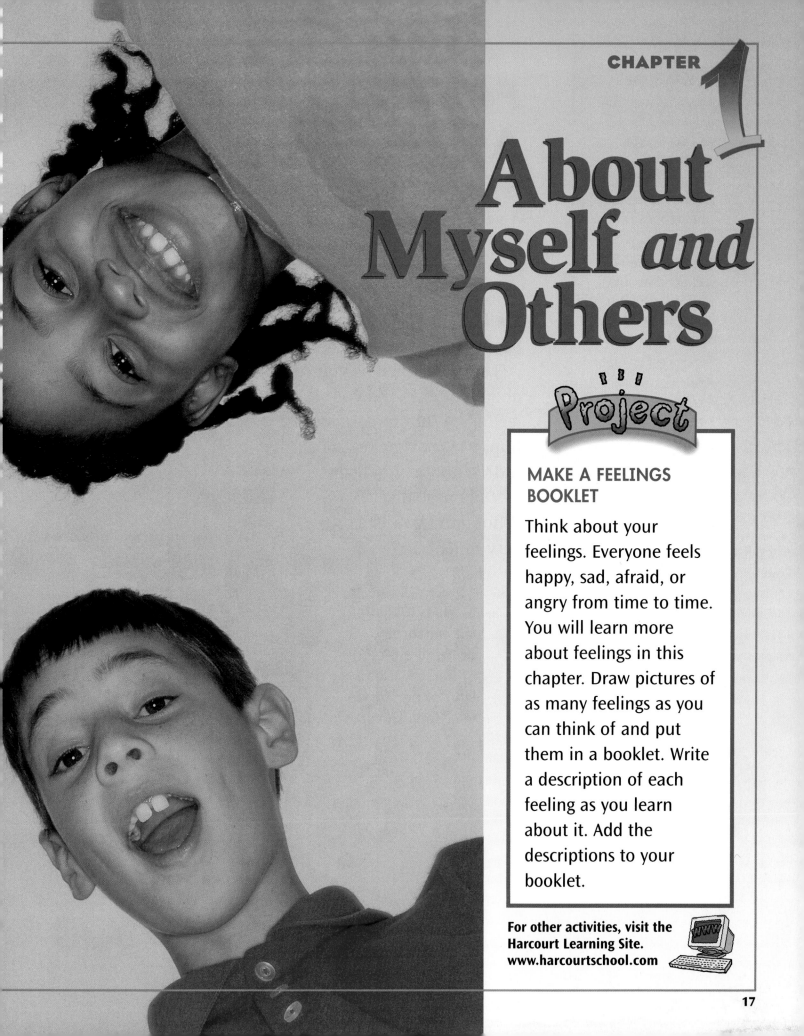

CHAPTER 1

About Myself and Others

Project

MAKE A FEELINGS BOOKLET

Think about your feelings. Everyone feels happy, sad, afraid, or angry from time to time. You will learn more about feelings in this chapter. Draw pictures of as many feelings as you can think of and put them in a booklet. Write a description of each feeling as you learn about it. Add the descriptions to your booklet.

For other activities, visit the Harcourt Learning Site.
www.harcourtschool.com

Feeling Good About Myself

MAIN IDEA
Treating yourself like a good friend is a way to respect yourself.

WHY LEARN THIS? When you feel good about who you are, it is easier to be happy and get along better.

VOCABULARY
- feelings
- respect
- responsible
- honest

Look in the mirror. Whose face do you see? A very special person is looking back at you. In the whole world there is no one else just like you.

Your feelings make you special. **Feelings** are the way you react to people and events.

Learn as much as you can about yourself and your feelings. What makes you happy? What makes you sad? What do you like best about yourself? What don't you like very much?

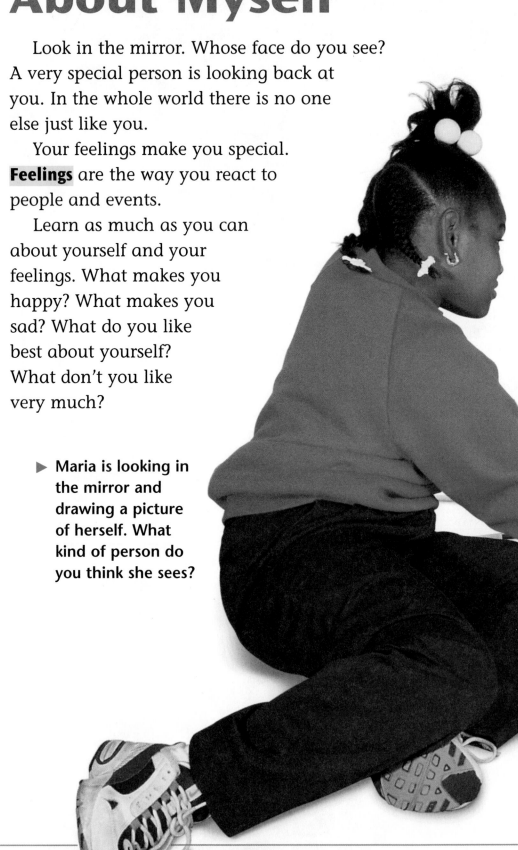

▶ Maria is looking in the mirror and drawing a picture of herself. What kind of person do you think she sees?

It is important to treat yourself like the special person you are. Treat yourself the same way you would treat a good friend. This means you feel proud of yourself when you do something well.

Being a friend to yourself also means you respect yourself. If you **respect** (rih•SPEKT) yourself, you believe in yourself. You stand up for yourself. You listen to your feelings and take good care of yourself.

Taking care of yourself shows you are learning to be responsible. Being **responsible** (rih•SPAHNT•suh•buhl) means that other people can count on you. It also means that you are **honest**—you tell the truth. Being responsible is a sign of growing up.

LESSON CHECKUP

Check Your Facts

1. What are feelings?
2. What can you do to be a good friend to yourself?
3. CRITICAL THINKING Give an example of something you could do that shows you respect yourself.

Set Health Goals

4. Name one way you have been responsible at school today. Name another way you can be responsible today.

MAIN IDEA
You can choose how to show your feelings. You can also decide how to express what you are feeling.

WHY LEARN THIS? Knowing as much as you can about your feelings is an important part of growing up.

VOCABULARY
• body language
• emotions
• self-control

Understanding My Feelings

Your feelings are a part of what makes you a special person. You choose when and how to express your feelings. Learning to name your feelings and express them in a safe way shows that you are growing up.

Where do my feelings come from?

Sometimes feelings come from an event. You are happy working on a project with friends. Feelings also come from thinking about an event in the past. You feel sad thinking back to the day you moved. You also have feelings about events to come. You are excited for winter vacation to arrive.

▼ Working in a group can be a lot of fun. How do you think these children feel as they practice their math skills together?

"All right!"

How do I show feelings?

You show your feelings in different ways. One way is through your words. Actions are another way to show feelings. When you cry, you may be saying you are sad, hurt, or angry. When you pet your dog, you are showing how much you care. Writing a thank-you note expresses your feelings in actions *and* in words!

Did you know that your body helps you show your feelings? Your face often tells others how you are feeling. A big smile lets people know that you are happy. Other parts of your body express your feelings, too. Your **body language** is how your body shows your feelings.

When your face gets red, your body is saying you are embarrassed or shy. If you say you aren't afraid, but your hands are shaking, your body is telling the truth for you.

When you know and can name a feeling, it is easier to choose how to express it. When feelings take you by surprise, they can explode out of you in words or actions. They can make you feel uncomfortable or not in control. This can be scary.

JOURNAL

In your Health Journal describe a time when you felt happy. How did you express it in words, in your actions, and in body language?

How can I control my feelings?

Everybody has a wide range of **emotions** (ih•MOH•shuhnz), or strong feelings. Emotions such as love and joy are nice to have. But emotions such as sadness and anger don't feel so comfortable.

When you have **self-control**, or power over your emotions, you can usually deal with unpleasant emotions. If you pay attention to your unpleasant emotions, they may go away faster.

The first step to self-control is finding the best word to describe the way you're feeling. You may be sad but an even better word might be lonely. When you know that you are lonely, you can make choices about how to express that feeling.

▼ **People of all ages have feelings. How do babies show that they are hungry, tired, or bored? As children get older, they learn words to tell how they feel. They also begin to find ways to control their feelings.**

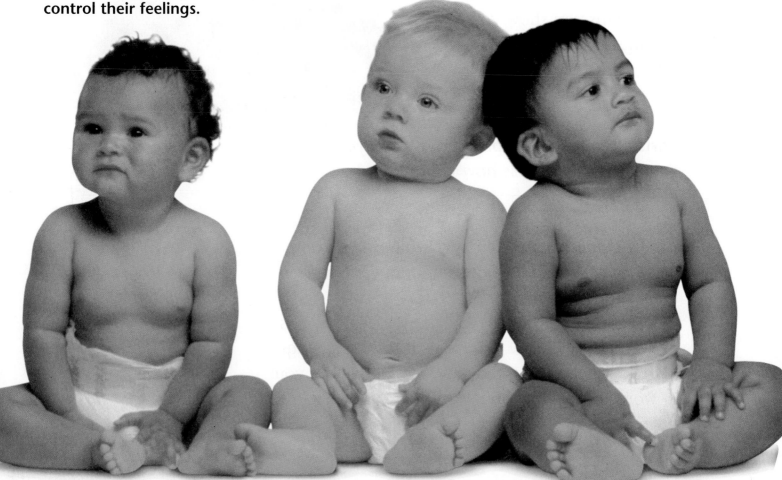

You may decide to go to your room and feel lonely for a while. You might want to talk to a family member or close friend. You may want to write in your journal.

After a while you may be tired of feeling lonely. You might be ready to do something about how you are feeling.

There are many ways to let go of emotions of all kinds. You can forgive yourself or someone else for what happened. You can get some exercise. You can read a book that makes you laugh. You can think of something new to do. You can call a friend. What do you do to let go of an unpleasant feeling?

Activity **Do Something About Your Feelings** Make a list of all the ways you can do something about unpleasant feelings such as boredom, anger, loneliness, and sadness. Draw a picture to show your best idea.

LESSON CHECKUP

Check Your Facts

❶ What are three different ways you show your feelings?

❷ What is self-control?

❸ Give three examples of expressing yourself through body language.

❹ CRITICAL THINKING Imagine that you are feeling sad. What is something you could do to make that feeling go away?

Set Health Goals

❺ Imagine that you are angry with a friend because she didn't return a book she borrowed. You are not in control of your emotions. What could you do to control the way you're feeling?

MAIN IDEA
You can learn how to deal with unpleasant feelings such as fear, stress, anger, and grief.

WHY LEARN THIS? When you know about unpleasant feelings, you can make wise choices about how to deal with them.

VOCABULARY
• fear
• stress
• anger
• grief

I'm afraid!

Dealing with Fear, Stress, Anger, and Grief

It is important to learn as much as you can about unpleasant feelings. Understanding them will make it easier to help yourself or a friend deal with one of these feelings.

How can I deal with fear?

There are many reasons you might feel **fear**, or be scared.

• You are in a new school or class.

• You are alone in your house.

• Some older children bully you.

When you feel afraid, your heart beats faster. You are nervous and upset. It is important to trust how you feel and to do something about it. It is part of being a good friend to yourself.

You can deal with some fears by yourself. If you are afraid of missing the school bus, you can set your alarm so you get up earlier. Other fears may be much more serious. Sometimes you need to talk to a trusted adult right away.

WHEN TO ASK FOR HELP

• Something makes you feel uncomfortable or scared.
• You are afraid to go to school.
• You have trouble sleeping.
• Someone touches you in a way you don't like.

How can I deal with stress?

When you feel **stress**, you may have butterflies in your stomach. Your hands may sweat. Your heart may even beat fast.

It is important to know why you are feeling stress. Are you afraid of a bully? Is there not enough time to finish your homework? If you have felt stress for a long time, you should talk to a parent or a trusted adult. He or she may have ideas to help you.

There are many ways to deal with stress. One way is to manage your time. First, make a list of what you have to do. Then, write down how long each task will take. Other ways to deal with stress are listed in the table.

CONSUMER FOCUS

Making Buying Decisions
Sometimes you can deal with stress by working on a hobby. Think of a hobby you have or would like to have, such as painting or fishing. Make a list of the items you would need to work on or start your hobby. Use the steps on page *xiv* to help you to find the best prices for these items.

• • •

DEAL WITH STRESS

- Talk to a family member or an adult.
- Plan your time wisely.
- Set goals you can reach.
- Get some exercise or work on a hobby.

How can I deal with angry, hurt, or sad feelings?

FOCUS

Communicate

Murray feels angry because his brother left the tops off his colored markers. He feels like telling his brother, "You are so stupid." Suggest a better way for Murray to tell his brother how he feels.
Use the steps for communicating shown on page *xii*. What if he began by saying "I feel . . ."?

• • •

When you feel **anger**, you are very mad. It is all right to be angry. Everyone gets angry sometimes. You may get angry if you don't get your way or if someone teases you. Hurt and sadness are other common feelings. You may feel hurt if you are blamed for something you didn't do. You may feel sad if your best friend moves away.

You can learn to manage your anger in ways that keep you safe and in control. You can learn to make wise choices about how you show your anger. Then you can decide what you want to do.

MANAGE ANGER
1. Stop what you are doing.
2. Count to ten to cool down or take three long, slow breaths.
3. Think about what is happening.
4. Take action. Either walk away or tell the person what you are feeling.
5. Use messages that tell how you feel. Begin with "I feel . . ."

I'm angry!

I'm hurt!

I'm sad

How can I deal with grief?

When you feel **grief**, you feel a deep sadness. This sadness may last for a while.

You may feel grief when a person or a pet dies. You may feel like being alone, or you may feel like crying. It is important to find a way to express your feelings.

Talking about how you feel is another way to express your grief. Family members, a teacher, and a member of the clergy are people who will listen to you. You can also take care of yourself by exercising, eating well, and getting enough sleep.

You can write a poem in your journal or draw a picture that expresses your sadness. Did you know that many famous artists express their feelings of grief and sadness in their artwork?

▶ Visual artists express their feelings through art.

Career

Visual Artist

What They Do

Visual artists include painters, illustrators, photographers, and sculptors. Visual artists express many different ideas and feelings in their artwork. A painter may express grief by doing a painting in memory of a person who died.

Education and Training

Some visual artists go to art school. Others learn and practice on their own. Some visual artists teach art classes for children or adults.

LESSON CHECKUP

Check Your Facts

❶ When should you ask for help if you are scared?

❷ CRITICAL THINKING How can planning ahead help you feel less stress?

❸ How can you express your anger but stay in control?

❹ Who can help you deal with grief?

Use Life Skills

❺ COMMUNICATE Pretend that you are angry with a friend who broke your favorite toy. How could you manage your anger in a way that keeps you in control?

MANAGE STRESS
at School

Everyone faces stress from time to time. Learning the following steps will help you handle your stress in a healthful way.

Learn This Skill

Tran's class is having a spelling bee next week. He is worried that he will be one of the first students to miss a word. How can Tran handle the stress he feels?

1. Know what stress feels like and what causes it.

Tran cannot fall asleep. He can feel his heart pounding and his muscles tightening. He is worried about the spelling bee.

2. When you feel stress, think about ways to handle it.

"My dad says I should make a list of what I need to do to get ready for the spelling bee."

3. Focus on one step at a time.

p-e-s-P-e-c-t

"Dad and I made a list of the words I still need to work on."

4. Learn to relax.

Tran takes a deep breath. "I am prepared, and I know that I will do my best!" he tells himself.

Practice This Skill

Use this summary to help you solve the problems below.

Steps for Managing Stress

1. Know what stress feels like and what causes it.

2. When you feel stress, think about ways to handle it.

3. Focus on one step at a time.

4. Learn to relax.

A. Sara is joining a Little League team. She has heard people say mean things to players who make mistakes. What can Sara do to deal with her fear about making a mistake?

B. Luis didn't do his homework because he left his math book at school. He is worried that his teacher will call on him. What should Luis do?

MAIN IDEA
Having good relationships with family and friends helps you have healthy relationships with other people.

WHY LEARN THIS? Getting along with family members and friends makes you feel good about yourself.

VOCABULARY
• relationship
• peers
• peer pressure

Relationships with Family and Friends

A **relationship** (rih•LAY•shuhn•ship) is the way you get along with someone. You spend a lot of time with your family and friends. It is important to get along well. When you have good relationships with your family and friends, it makes you feel good about yourself.

What makes good relationships with family?

Each person in a family has a special role. It is important to respect everyone in your family—from the youngest to the oldest. Talking and listening to all family members are ways of showing respect.

▼ How would you describe the relationships of the family members in these four photos?

Families work together better when family members respect and trust each other. When you tell the truth, you let your family members know they can trust you.

Being a responsible family member makes you feel good about yourself. It also lets your family know that they can depend on you to do your part. It means you are growing up. Some people your age do the dishes, set the table, take out the trash, or care for a pet. What chores do you do at home?

Families need time to play together, too. When you and your family have a good time together, it reminds you of how special it is to be a family. Some families like to ride bikes, make pizza, play games, or plan surprises together.

All families have problems at times. That's when family members need to work together and support each other. Taking time to talk together about what each family member can do helps families feel close. It's another way for family members to show they care about each other.

Gaining Attention

You know that babies cry to get attention when they are hungry or need to be changed. What are some acceptable ways you can get attention at home and at school? Make a list and share it with a classmate. Discuss your lists and make changes if necessary. Then share your lists as a class.

○ ○ ○

What do you like to do with your family?

What makes good relationships with friends?

Roller skating, birthday parties, school projects, and playing sports are fun ways to be with friends. Even doing a chore such as raking leaves is more fun with a friend!

Do you like to swim or build models? It's fun to find friends who like the same things you do. School clubs, neighborhood centers, and church groups can be good places to see old friends and make new friends.

Sometimes, however, even best friends disagree. When you and a friend don't agree, try to listen and talk things over. Say you're sorry if you do something that hurts a friend. Be ready to forgive your friend if he or she hurts you. Sometimes others do not know that their actions affect you.

Myth and Fact

Myth: Your friends will like you better if you always go along with them.

Fact: Your true friends will respect you for standing up for what you believe in.

• • • • • • • •

► How are these children enjoying their friendship?

◀ Friends can have differences and still have many things in common.

It's important to have **peers**—friends your age—who share your interests. However, if some of your friends want you to do something just because "everyone is doing it," they are using **peer pressure**. If it doesn't feel right to you, or it is against your family rules, stand up for yourself and make another choice. When you do that, you can be proud of yourself. It's a sign that you respect yourself and your family. You are also setting a good example for your peers.

LESSON CHECKUP

Check Your Facts

1 How can you show respect for each member of your family? How can family members show respect for you?

2 What jobs can children your age do to be responsible family members?

3 What are some ways to meet new friends?

4 CRITICAL THINKING Why is it important to be able to talk over problems with your friends?

Set Health Goals

5 Give an example of peer pressure. Describe what you could do to stand up for yourself.

MAIN IDEA
Speaking and listening respectfully to others helps you understand yourself and others better.

WHY LEARN THIS? You can use what you learn to improve your listening and communication skills.

VOCABULARY
• communicate
• compassion
• apologize

Communicating Well with Others

To **communicate** (kuh•MYOO•nuh•kayt) means to share information. You can learn to communicate in a way that helps you understand yourself and others better.

Using I-messages helps communicate your feelings. "I feel bad when you don't keep a promise" is an I-message. It helps others understand your feelings. It gives them a chance to respond.

It is important to take turns listening and speaking. When others are speaking, listen carefully so you can understand them. Listening carefully, even when you disagree, is a way to respect other people.

If you have **compassion** (kuhm•PA•shuhn), you can feel what others feel. You treat people in a kind and caring way. You don't use put-downs or act like a bully, because you want to show respect and communicate well.

▶ There are many ways for friends to communicate.

▲ These brothers are communicating with a friend who lives far away. How else could they communicate with him?

When you are wrong, you should **apologize** (uh•PAH•luh•jyz)—say you are sorry. You are asking the other person to forgive you. When people tell you they are sorry, you can forgive them.

Using words to communicate your feelings and listening respectfully to other people are signs that you are becoming more responsible.

Activity **Use Communication Skills** Choose one of the pictures on these pages. Write a paragraph about the picture. Include how these friends are using good communication skills.

LIFE SKILLS
FOCUS

Communicate

A friend told someone else something about you that is not true. Tell how you can communicate your feelings by using I-messages. Use the steps for communicating shown on page *xii*.

• • •

LESSON CHECKUP

Check Your Facts

❶ Name four helpful communication skills.

❷ CRITICAL THINKING Why might you apologize to a friend?

Set Health Goals

❸ Which communication skill is easiest for you? Which communication skill is the hardest for you? Describe a time when communication skills might come in handy.

RESOLVE CONFLICTS
with Friends

Ignoring how other people feel can lead to conflicts. Learning how to resolve conflicts will help you have more healthful relationships.

Learn This Skill

Some of the students are making fun of Martha, the new girl, because she wears glasses. When Dennis arrives, they expect him to join in. Dennis wants to go along with his friends, but he knows that teasing is wrong. What should Dennis do?

1. Use I-messages to tell how you feel.

"I feel sad when Martha is teased," says Dennis.

2. Listen to each other.

"You may think what you are saying is funny, but it isn't funny if it makes someone sad." "We weren't trying to be mean," the group replies.

3. Think of the other person's point of view.

"Look—Martha's new. That's hard enough. Let's include her in our group."

4. Decide what to do.

"Dennis is right—let's all try to get to know each other."

Practice This Skill

Use this summary to help you solve the problems below.

Steps for Resolving Conflicts

1. Use I-messages to tell how you feel.

2. Listen to each other.

3. Think of the other person's point of view.

4. Decide what to do.

A. Your friend's parents say it's OK to walk to the store. You want to go, but you know your parents wouldn't want you to. Explain how you feel and why you can't go.

B. You are the youngest one on a family vacation. Your parents want you to go to bed earlier than everyone else. Write down why your parents might think you need to go to bed early.

USE VOCABULARY

anger (p. 26)

apologize (p. 35)

body language (p. 21)

communicate (p. 34)

compassion (p. 34)

emotions (p. 22)

fear (p. 24)

feelings (p. 18)

grief (p. 27)

honest (p. 19)

peer pressure (p. 33)

peers (p. 33)

relationship (p. 30)

respect (p. 19)

responsible (p. 19)

self-control (p. 22)

stress (p. 25)

Use the terms above to complete the sentences. Page numbers in ( ) tell you where to look in the chapter if you need help.

1. Friends your own age are ____.

2. To ____ means to share information.

3. ____ are strong feelings.

4. If you feel ____, you are very mad.

5. When you say you are sorry, you ____.

6. Being ____ means that other people can count on you.

7. When you feel ____, you may have butterflies in your stomach.

8. If you have ____, you can feel what others feel.

9. ____ are the way you react to people and events.

10. When you are ____, you tell the truth.

11. ____ is a deep sadness.

12. A ____ is the way you get along with someone.

13. If you ____ yourself, you believe in yourself.

14. Your ____ is how your body shows your feelings.

15. ____ may cause you to do something because "everyone is doing it."

16. If you have power over your emotions, you have ____.

17. If you feel ____, you are afraid.

CHECK YOUR FACTS

Page numbers in ( ) tell you where to look in the chapter if you need help.

18. What is an I-message? (p. 34)

19. What are three ways to let go of emotions? (p. 23)

20. Name two things you can do to be a good friend to yourself. (p. 19)

21. What are two things you can do when you and a friend disagree? (p. 32)

22. Name four things you can do to deal with stress. (p. 25)

 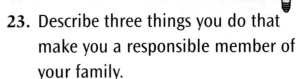

23. Describe three things you do that make you a responsible member of your family.

24. Pretend that you are sad because your best friend is moving away. How would you express your sadness in your words, actions, and body language?

APPLY LIFE SKILLS

25. **Manage Stress** Suppose you are worried about a math test you will have tomorrow. Write the steps for managing stress and tell how you can deal with the stress you feel.

26. **Resolve Conflicts** Suppose you and a friend have a disagreement because he wants you to play baseball instead of finishing your homework. Write the steps for resolving conflicts and tell how you can work out your disagreement.

Promote Health **Home and Community**

1. Talk with family members about things all of you do to get along with each other.
2. Make a poster that shows at least four important communication skills. Display it at your school or at home.

Activities

Mirror, Mirror, on the Wall

On Your Own • Look in the mirror and study your face. Imagine that you are angry. How does your face look? Now imagine that you are about to go to the beach with your family. How does your face look now? Draw pictures of yourself showing each of these emotions.

Getting to Know You

With a Team • On poster board write down five things you could do to get to know a new student. Draw pictures to go with your words.

Communicating Your Feelings

With a Partner • Imagine that you and a friend have a disagreement over which game to play. Write down at least four I-messages you could use to help you communicate your feelings. Take turns reading your I-messages.

Managing Your Time

At Home • Imagine that you never have time to finish all your chores. Make a time management chart to help you.

Multiple Choice

Choose the letter of the correct answer.

1. You can show your feelings through
   _____ .
   a. actions
   b. words
   c. body language
   d. all of these

2. You're feeling _____ when you have butterflies in your stomach and your hands are sweaty.
   a. stress   b. grief
   c. anger   d. sadness

3. It's important to have good _____ with family members and friends.
   a. responsibility   b. emotion
   c. relationships   d. feeling

4. Using I-messages helps you _____ your feelings.
   a. respect   b. communicate
   c. forgive   d. apologize

Modified True or False

Write *true* or *false*. If a sentence is false, replace the underlined term to make the sentence true.

5. Taking care of yourself shows that you are learning to be <u>responsible</u>.

6. Having <u>self-control</u> over your emotions can help you deal with unpleasant feelings.

7. Families work together better when family members <u>respect</u> each other.

8. It is <u>not all right</u> to feel angry.

9. Your <u>feelings</u> are the way you respond to people and events.

10. Using <u>you-messages</u> is a good way to communicate your feelings.

11. Talking and listening to others is a way of showing <u>respect</u>.

Short Answer

Write a sentence to answer each item.

12. What are two things families might do when they have problems?

13. Name two things you do for yourself when you respect yourself.

14. Give an example of something you could do to show compassion.

15. Name three types of visual artists.

16. What are three things you can do to improve your communication?

Writing in Health

Write a paragraph to answer each item.

17. Luis feels lonely. What are three things he could do to let go of that feeling?

18. Roberta is feeling stress because she doesn't think she can finish her social studies project on time. How could she deal with her stress?

CHAPTER 2

Me and My Family

MAKE A FAMILY BOOK

Make a book titled "Things Families Do Together." Include fun things as well as jobs families might work on together, such as making meals.

For other activities, visit the Harcourt Learning Site.
www.harcourtschool.com

MAIN IDEA
Families enjoy working and playing together.

WHY LEARN THIS? When family members play and work well together, they learn to respect each other.

VOCABULARY
• family
• values

What Is a Family?

Your **family** is the group of people you live with. There are many kinds of families. Some families have children and two parents. Other families have one parent, a grandparent, or another adult. A stepparent or stepchildren may be part of a family. Who is in your family?

Your family makes sure your basic needs are met. They give you food, a place to sleep, and clothes to wear. They love you, help you when you are ill or scared, and make rules to keep you safe.

Families also teach values. **Values** (VAL•yooz) are strong beliefs, such as honesty and caring about others. Children first learn about right and wrong in their families.

Most parents love their children. They try hard to give their children what they need to grow up strong and healthy.

▼ There are many kinds of families.

▲ Family members can have fun together.

How does a family play together?

Family members can play together in many ways. Some families like to play sports or go hiking. Other families choose books to read out loud. Some work on jigsaw puzzles. Others play games or watch videos. How do the people in your family play together?

Playing together can make everyone in a family feel good. You laugh together as you plan a special surprise. You talk as you put together a puzzle. You have a chance to relax together as you ride bikes or walk the dog.

Playing together gives family members a chance to talk and listen to each other. You get to know each other better. You talk about what you are feeling. You learn to respect each other.

When members of a family have fun together, it makes everyone happy. It makes everyone glad to be part of the family.

LANGUAGE ARTS CONNECTION

"I'll Never Forget the Time . . ."

On Your Own Write a story about a funny or exciting time with your family that you will never forget. Tell what you liked best about the event.

○ ○ ○

How does a family work together?

It's important for family members to work together. When people in a family work together, it makes everyone in the family feel proud.

In some families the children are responsible for certain jobs. One child may always set the table, carry in firewood, or take care of a pet. In other families parents and children take turns doing some jobs, such as washing the dishes or taking out the trash.

You may have different jobs depending on where your family lives. If you live in a city apartment, you will have different jobs from someone who lives on a farm.

Taking Care of Maggie

1. Feed her. ✓
2. Give her clean water. ✓
3. Pet her. ✓
4. Brush her for 10 minutes. ○
5. Keep her litter box clean. ✓

◀ **Taking care of a pet is a good way to show responsibility.**

I'll help!

Activity **Think of New Jobs** List the ways you help your family. What three new ways could you add to your list?

It feels good to be a responsible member of your family. You are being responsible when you do a job without waiting to be asked. For example you can keep your room clean or offer to help with big jobs.

When everyone in a family works together, no one person has to do all the work. Jobs get done more quickly. And that leaves more time for play!

LESSON CHECKUP

Check Your Facts

1. How does your family meet your basic needs?
2. Name three reasons it's important for family members to play together.
3. CRITICAL THINKING What jobs could people in your family take turns doing?

Set Health Goals

4. Think of three things you would like to do with your family. Give other family members a chance to add to the list. With your family, choose an activity from the list, and make a plan for doing it.

Changes in Families

MAIN IDEA
All families go through changes. Some changes are harder than others.

WHY LEARN THIS? It helps to know ways that family members can help each other during good times and bad times.

VOCABULARY
• divorce
• sibling

Have you ever seen a snow globe—a glass ball that "snows" when you turn it upside down? When big changes happen in a family, you may feel as if you're inside a snow globe. Everything may suddenly seem to be turning upside down.

What happens when families change?

Changes happen all the time. Many changes are fun, but some are hard. Moving, divorce or remarriage, a new baby, and the death of a pet are all big changes. Everyone in the family will need time to get used to changes like these.

Moving to a new place can feel confusing. If you move, you may feel sad about leaving your old friends and your old home. But you may also feel excited about going to a new school.

Moving day can bring mixed feelings.

48

Activity **Write About Change** These snow globes show big changes that can turn a family upside down for a time. Choose one, or think of another big change. Write about all the feelings you might have as you get used to the change.

When parents **divorce** (duh•VORS), it means they are no longer married to each other. If parents divorce or remarry, it is normal to feel sad, scared, and confused for a while.

When a pet dies, you may feel sad a long time. Even if you get another pet, you will always remember the pet that died.

When a new baby joins your family, you have a new brother or sister, or **sibling**. You may feel excited but also jealous of the time your parents spend with the baby. It may take some time for you to get to know your new brother or sister.

If a big change happens in your family, it's all right to feel whatever you are feeling. Be patient with yourself and with other family members.

How can family members help each other?

JOURNAL

Make notes in your Health Journal about how you and your family work as a team. How can you help your family in new ways? Remember that your journal is private. You do not have to share it with classmates.

When you were little, your parents did everything for you. Now that you are older, you can begin to help them. When family members help each other, they feel as if they're part of the same team.

It's easier for a family to be a good team when family members share the same values. If all the people in your family speak politely to each other and tell the truth, it helps your family stay strong.

Family rules also help family members work as a team. When all the people in your family respect the rules, family members argue less often and have more fun together.

Team members help each other. You may help by reading stories to a younger sibling. Sometimes the whole family might pitch in for a big project such as painting the house. By helping, you are being a responsible member of your family.

◀ Reading a book out loud is a good way to spend time with a younger sibling.

▲ **Mealtime is a good time for family members to listen to each other's ideas and feelings.**

LIFE SKILLS
FOCUS

Resolve Conflicts

Your younger brother and sister always interrupt when you are talking. This makes you angry. How can you help them learn to listen politely and wait their turn to speak? Use the steps for resolving conflicts shown on page *xiii*.

For a family to be a good team, family members need to communicate. It takes practice to learn to talk and listen respectfully to each family member. Some families spend time talking while eating meals, riding in the car, or making breakfast.

When family members can talk to each other, work together, and have fun together, they feel like a team. They feel close to each other. Feeling close makes it easier for family members to help each other when big changes happen.

LESSON CHECKUP

Check Your Facts

❶ Name some times when all the members of a family can talk together.

❷ What kinds of feelings might you have when a new sibling is born?

❸ CRITICAL THINKING How are family team rules like a sports team's rules?

❹ Why are family rules important?

Set Health Goals

❺ Write one goal you would like your family to work toward. What could each family member do to help?

COMMUNICATE
with Family Members

Even when planning fun activities, family members need to communicate with each other. This skill will help you do just that.

Learn This Skill

Jenny's family is planning which restaurant to go to on Friday night. Each family member gets to present an idea.

1. Understand your audience.

Jenny knows each family member has certain likes and dislikes. They will have to work together to choose a restaurant all will accept.

2. Give a clear message.

Jenny says that she loves Mexican food and that she'd like to go to the Mexican Fiesta.

3. Listen.

Jenny listens to the rest of the family. Her brother says they eat Mexican food too often. He wants to go to the Little Italy restaurant.

4. Gather feedback.

Everyone talks and listens. They decide to go Italian this Friday and Mexican next Friday.

Practice This Skill

Use the steps to help you solve the problems.

> ### Communicating with Family Members
> 1. Understand your audience.   3. Listen.
> 2. Give a clear message.   4. Gather feedback.

A. Kathy gets angry when her brother borrows her bike without asking. How can Kathy communicate her feelings to her brother?

B. Larry is upset. His sister promised to help him clean the kitchen, and then she forgot. How can Larry communicate how he feels?

MAIN IDEA As you develop from a baby into an adult, you go through four stages of growth.

WHY LEARN THIS? Learning about how people grow helps you understand the changes you will go through.

VOCABULARY
• life cycle

Everyone Grows and Changes

The Human Life Cycle

birth to two

two to ten

ten to adult

adult to senior

▲ Birth to two

What is the human life cycle?

The next time you're at the mall, look around. You will see babies, children, teenagers, and adults. Each group is in a different stage of the life cycle. The human **life cycle** includes four stages of growth that people go through.

Birth to Two During the first stage of growth in the human life cycle, you were a tiny, helpless baby. You were not able to care for yourself. To stay alive, you had to be cared for by your parents or other adults.

During this first stage of your life, you grew at an amazing rate. From before you were born until about age two, you grew faster than you ever will again. You changed from a baby into an active, more independent two-year-old.

Two to Ten Between the ages of two and ten, you grow more slowly. You grow only about 2 or 3 inches a year.

Your language skills develop quickly during this stage. Now you can read and write. You can use your thinking skills to solve problems.

You can run faster and throw a ball farther than ever before. You can put your physical and mental skills together to learn a complex task, such as riding a bicycle.

▼ Two to ten

Career

Pediatrician

What They Do

Pediatricians are doctors who take care of babies and children. Your parents probably took you to a pediatrician for many checkups when you were a baby. You were measured and weighed to make sure you were healthy and growing normally. Pediatricians make sure children have their vaccinations. They also help children get better when they are ill. Pediatricians may see the same children from the time they are babies until they are adults.

Education and Training

Pediatricians go to college for four years and medical school for four more years. After they go through training in pediatrics for three more years, they can practice medicine.

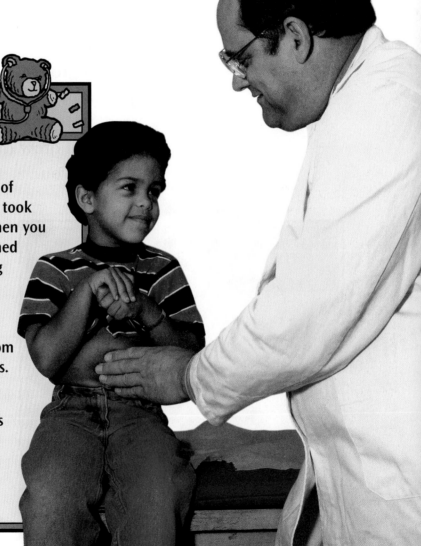

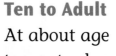

▶ **Ten to adult**

Ten to Adult

At about age ten or twelve, you will enter the next stage of growth. You will begin to change from a child into an adult. As a teenager you will again grow very fast. Your body will become taller and heavier.

This growth stage usually happens sooner for girls than for boys, but boys catch up and often grow faster at about age fourteen or fifteen. Your body will grow and change when it is the right time for you.

Adult to Senior When you are an adult, you will stop growing taller. As an adult you will decide what kind of job you want to have, whether or not you will get married, and whether or not you will have children. As an older adult, or senior, you will have more free time to learn new things and to enjoy your family and friends.

◀ **Adult to senior**

younger

older

younger

older

JOURNAL

Ask family members to tell you their favorite stories about things you did when you were a baby. Choose your favorite story, and write it in your Health Journal.

Activity **See How You've Changed** What can the older children in these photos do that they needed help with when they were younger? Make a list of things you needed help with when you were younger.

Remember when you were a baby?

You probably don't remember yourself as a tiny baby, but this is what you were like. You had a large head and wobbly legs. You could grasp a finger and suck to get milk, but adults had to take care of you.

Your fastest growth period began before you were born and lasted until you were two. Your body and brain grew quickly. By the age of two, you could sit up, walk, and talk. Look at pictures of yourself as a baby. Think of all the ways you have changed since then!

LESSON CHECKUP

Check Your Facts

1 During which two stages of the human life cycle do you grow most quickly?

2 CRITICAL THINKING What kinds of decisions will you make when you are an adult? What do you think you'll decide to do?

3 What skills do you learn during your second stage of growth?

Set Health Goals

4 List three things you can do now that you couldn't do three years ago. Now list three things you hope to do three years from now.

People Grow at Different Rates

MAIN IDEA Cells have important jobs to do. When cells divide and multiply, you grow.

WHY LEARN THIS? Learning how you grow helps you understand why it is important to take care of your body.

VOCABULARY
• cell
• tissues
• organs
• organ system
• growth rate

How do people grow?

Everything from your nose to your toes grows because of the tiny cells inside you. A **cell** is the smallest working part of your body. Your growth began with one cell. Now you have many cells. During periods of rapid growth, the cells inside your body multiply quickly.

Your bones, skin, blood, and muscles are all made up of cells. Cells contain information your body needs to be able to eat, breathe, and think. By taking good care of your body, you help your cells do their important work.

Activity **List Differences** Each person starts out as one cell, yet no two people are alike. List ten ways you are different from the people in the photo and from anyone else you know.

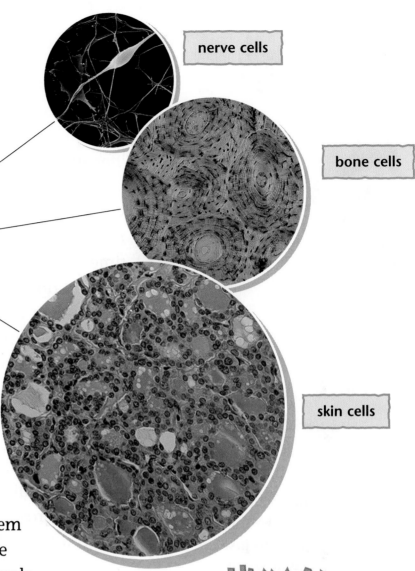

nerve cells

bone cells

skin cells

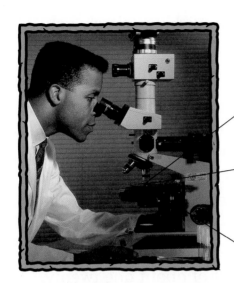

▲ You need a microscope to see most cells. Each cell's shape helps it do its job.

What do cells do?

Cells come in different shapes and sizes that help them do special jobs. Nerve cells are long and thin. They carry signals through your body. Bone cells surround themselves with a hard material. They help hold your body up. Skin cells are flat. They form layers to protect and cover your body.

Cells that work together to get a job done are called **tissues** (TIH•shooz). Muscle tissue is one kind of tissue in your body. Groups of tissues join together to form **organs**. Your heart is one of your organs. It is made up of different tissues that work together to pump blood through your whole body. Many organs work together in an **organ system**. Your blood, heart, and all your blood vessels together make up your circulatory system.

HUMAN BODY CONNECTION

Examine Organ Systems

Look through the organ systems, also called body systems, on pages 1–15. Pick one organ in each system, and tell what it does.

● ● ●

"We all grow at our own rate."

What is the special way you grow?

Your **growth rate** is how quickly or slowly you grow. Everyone goes through the same basic periods of growth, but each person's growth rate is different.

From before birth to age two, you grew very quickly. Your family can tell you how much you changed in a short amount of time when you were a baby. As a teenager you will again grow quickly. In between, your growth rate will be very slow. By the time you are an adult of about age twenty, you will stop growing taller.

Sometimes you may compare yourself to your friends and wonder if you are normal. You may worry that you are growing too much or not enough. Remember, no two people are alike. And there is no one way to grow. You grow in your own time and at your own speed to the height that is right for you.

▲ Have fun and don't worry! Your body is growing just the way it should.

CONSUMER FOCUS

Access Valid Health Information

Sylvie's mom buys foods to help Sylvie grow up to be healthy. Sylvie's mom knows foods with calcium will help Sylvie's bones to be strong. Use the steps on page *xvi* to research what calcium is and why it helps Sylvie's bones grow strong.

• • •

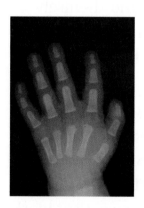 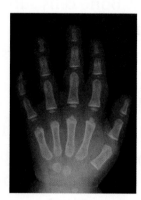 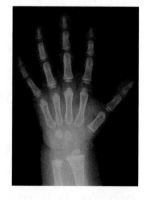

| birth | twelve months | eighteen months |

▲ Growth happens all through your body. When you were born, you had no wrist bones. But they developed by the time you were eighteen months (one and a half years) old.

| six months | one year | three years | five years | seven years | ten years |

▲ A newborn baby's head is very large. As a person grows, the body gets bigger, but the head size remains about the same.

You grow because the cells inside you divide to make many new cells. You add inches to your height as your bones get longer. You grow stronger as your muscles stretch to cover your growing bones. You also add weight to your body.

Your physical growth is easy to see, but you are growing in other ways, too. As your brain cells grow larger and make new connections, you learn new things. You can think about and solve harder problems. You can begin to be more responsible for yourself. People can count on you in new ways.

LESSON CHECKUP

Check Your Facts

1. What happens when cells multiply and make many new cells?

2. Why are cells different shapes?

3. CRITICAL THINKING Do you ever stop growing?

4. Tell how cells, tissues, organs, and organ systems are related.

Set Health Goals

5. Name two ways your growth can let you be a more responsible family member.

Taking Care of My Body

MAIN IDEA
Your body has important jobs to do. When you take good care of your body, you can grow and develop in healthful ways.

WHY LEARN THIS? Taking good care of your body helps you grow strong and healthy.

VOCABULARY
• private

The best way to grow healthy and strong is to take good care of your body. When you feel well, your body is telling you that you are doing a good job of taking care of it. When you feel tired or weak, or if you are often ill, your body may be telling you to make some changes.

Getting regular exercise and eating a balanced diet are important. Your body also needs to rest. With enough sleep you will be ready for the day ahead. Keeping your body, hair, nails, and teeth clean is important, too. You will learn more about exercise and diet in Chapters 3 and 4 of this book.

Support good health habits!

Eat healthful foods!

Get regular checkups!

Get plenty of rest!

Be vaccinated against disease!

Keep your body clean!

Exercise!

You may have a box of special treasures that you keep **private**, which means they belong only to you. Each family member has a right to private things. You need to respect the privacy of others. Knock before entering a room. Ask before using things that belong to someone else.

Your body is special. There are parts of your body you have a right to keep private. It feels good to get a hug from someone you trust. A pat on the back for a job well done makes you feel great. But there are some touches that don't feel good. It is not proper for someone to touch you on a private part of your body or in a way that makes you feel uncomfortable. Talk to a trusted adult if this happens.

When You Need Help, Talk to a Trusted Adult
- Parent
- Teacher
- Doctor
- Religious leader
- Counselor
- Nurse
- Police officer

▶ **A kind touch on the shoulder can make someone feel better.**

LESSON CHECKUP

Check Your Facts

1. Why is it important to take good care of your body?
2. Tell where to get help with a problem.

Use Life Skills

3. MAKE DECISIONS Imagine that your friend invites you over to have ice cream. You want to go, but you haven't eaten dinner yet. Use your decision-making skills to make a healthful choice.

USE VOCABULARY

cell (p. 58)   growth rate (p. 60)   organs (p. 59)   tissues (p. 59)

divorce (p. 49)   life cycle (p. 54)   private (p. 63)   values (p. 44)

family (p. 44)   organ system (p. 59)   sibling (p. 49)

Use the terms above to complete the sentences. Page numbers in ( ) tell you where to look in the chapter if you need help.

1. Your brother or sister is called your _____.

2. Tissues work together to form _____.

3. Your _____ is very fast between birth and two years of age.

4. Your growth began with one _____.

5. Birth to age two is one stage in the human _____.

6. When you keep something _____, it belongs only to you.

7. When parents _____, they are no longer married to each other.

8. Cells that work together are called _____.

9. Strong beliefs taught in families are called _____.

10. Your _____ is the group of people you live with.

11. Many organs work together to form a(n) _____.

CHECK YOUR FACTS

Page numbers in ( ) tell you where to look in the chapter if you need help.

12. Name three jobs you can do to help as a member of your family. (p. 46)

13. Name four big changes that can happen in families. (pp. 48–49)

14. List the four stages of growth in the human life cycle. (pp. 54–56)

15. Name the types of cells in the pictures shown here. (p. 59)

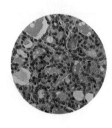

16. Name three good ways to take care of your body. (p. 62)

17. How can you respect each family member's right to privacy? How can family members respect yours?

18. Study the photo below. Why is it important to understand that all people grow at their own rates and in their own time?

19. Resolve Conflicts Suppose a friend invites you over on the night your family has planned to do something together. What will you say to your friend, and why?

20. Communicate Suppose someone touches you in a way that does not feel comfortable to you. What would you say or do, and why?

Promote Health — Home and Community

1. In your school, take a survey of the chores children do around the house. Sort the chores by grade level. Design and make a poster to show your results.

2. Make a growth chart, and ask your family members to record their heights on the chart each month for a year. Be sure to record your height, too. As each month passes, notice how much some family members are growing taller. At the end of the year, add up the number of inches each person grew. Use the numbers to show which stage of the life cycle each person is in.

Activities

At Home • Interview older family members, and list the jobs they did when they were your age. Which jobs are the same as the ones you do? Which are different?

Circles of Life

With a Team • Find out about the life cycles of other living things. How are their stages of growth the same as the stages in the human life cycle? How are they different?

Picture Perfect

With a Partner • Make a poster of the human life cycle. Draw a big circle, and divide it into four parts to represent each stage. Then cut out pictures, and paste them in each section. Be sure your chart shows how humans may look and what they may do at each stage of life.

Movin' On

On Your Own • Imagine that you have moved several times and you have been asked to help other children your age who are moving. Make a booklet suggesting ways to help them deal with the move.

Multiple Choice

Choose the letter of the correct answer.

1. Basic needs are met in your ____.
   a. club   b. family
   c. cells   d. life cycle

2. Your whole body is made up of ____.
   a. growth   b. cells
   c. organs   d. water

3. Cleaning your room shows you are ____.
   a. responsible b. healthy
   c. honest   d. happy

4. When tired, your body needs ____.
   a. food   b. exercise
   c. rest   d. water

5. Your first stage of growth ended at ____.
   a. two   b. adulthood
   c. twelve   d. sixteen

Modified True or False

Write *true* or *false*. If a sentence is false, replace the underlined term to make the sentence true.

6. Listening respectfully is a good way to communicate.

7. A new doctor causes family changes.

8. Tissues that work together form organs.

9. During the third stage of growth, you are becoming a senior.

10. A pediatrician is a doctor who specializes in the care of adults.

11. Families teach jobs, like honesty.

12. It is important to respect other people's privacy.

13. Teenagers grow at the same rates.

14. As an adult you make lots of decisions.

15. Once you are about twelve years old, you will not grow any taller.

Short Answer

Write a complete sentence to answer each question.

16. What important jobs do cells do?

17. Who can you talk to if someone touches you in a way that makes you uncomfortable?

18. How can families help each other?

19. List two skills that develop between the ages of two and ten.

20. If a younger sibling is having a hard day, how can you show you care?

Writing in Health

Write paragraphs to answer each item.

21. Describe what it feels like when big changes happen in families.

22. During the two-to-ten stage, many children learn to ride a bicycle. List some skills needed to ride a bike.

Keeping My Body Fit

PLAN A FITNESS GAME

Running, swimming, riding a bike, jumping rope, and even walking are different kinds of exercise. As you read through this chapter, you will learn that exercise is an important part of taking care of your body. Plan a fitness game for your class to play. Be sure your game includes several kinds of exercise that will help your body in different ways.

For other activities, visit the Harcourt Learning Site.
www.harcourtschool.com

MAIN IDEA
Caring for your skin helps you stay healthy.

WHY LEARN THIS? You can use what you learn to practice good skin care.

VOCABULARY
• pores
• bacteria
• sunscreen

HUMAN BODY CONNECTION

Under Your Skin

Your skin is more than a simple covering for your body. Turn to page 3 of The Amazing Human Body to find out what lies beneath the surface of your skin.

• • •

Caring for My Skin

Have you ever had an itchy rash? If so, you know skin problems can be annoying. You can't stop all skin problems. But you can stop many of them. Caring for your skin helps you stay healthy and look good too.

How can I keep my skin clean?

Do you know your skin has holes in it? These tiny holes are called **pores** (POHRZ). Sweat comes up through your pores. Sweat helps cool your body. Oil comes up to the surface of the skin along hairs. Oil helps keep your skin soft.

Oil, sweat, and dirt collect on your skin. Bacteria grow on your skin too. **Bacteria** (bak•TIR•ee•uh) are living things that are so tiny you cannot see them. Some bacteria cause illness. Washing with soap and warm water is the best way to get rid of oil, sweat, dirt, and bacteria on your skin.

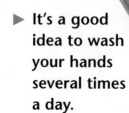

▶ It's a good idea to wash your hands several times a day.

Washing your hands is very important. When your hands are clean, you are less likely to catch or spread illnesses such as colds. Always wash your hands before you eat. Wash your hands after using the bathroom. Wash your hands right away if you sneeze or cough into them. If you touch an animal, wash your hands soon afterward.

To clean your whole body, take a bath or shower. Bathe whenever you are dirty or sweaty. Some people need to bathe every day. Others can skip a day if they don't get too dirty or sweaty.

▼ Bath time can be relaxing and fun. A back brush helps you wash hard-to-reach spots.

How can I protect my skin from the sun?

The sun gives off harmful rays. You cannot see the rays, but they can burn you. This kind of burn is called a sunburn. A sunburn goes away in a few days. The real harm from too much sun shows up years later. Skin may get tough. It may get very wrinkled. Skin cancer, a disease that can be deadly, may occur.

Skin damage can happen even if you never get a sunburn. It can happen if you get a tan. Everyone needs protection from the sun.

Everyone needs to use sunscreen!

▼ **How are these children protecting themselves from the sun?**

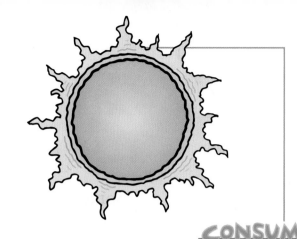

The sun is strongest in the middle of the day. So try to limit your time outdoors to early morning, late afternoon, or evening. If you do go out in the middle of the day, cover up. Your clothes will help protect you from the sun. Wear long sleeves and long pants. If it is hot, wear loose clothes that are light in weight and light colored. They will help you stay cool. Wear a hat to shade your face.

Rub sunscreen on any uncovered skin. **Sunscreen** is a lotion or cream that can protect you from the sun's harmful rays. Some sunscreens block almost all harmful rays. Other sunscreens give you just a little protection. Before you go outside, ask an adult in your family which sunscreen is best for you.

Your eyes also need protection from the sun. Over time the sun's rays can harm your eyes. Wearing sunglasses is the best way to protect them. Never look right at the sun, even if you're wearing sunglasses. With sunglasses, sunscreen, and the right clothing, you can have fun in the sun and still be safe.

CONSUMER FOCUS

Making Buying Decisions
How can you choose the best sunscreen? Find out what SPF means and choose the best SPF for you. Then compare several different sunscreen brands to decide which one is best for you and your family. Use page *xiv* to help you make your decision.

• • •

LESSON CHECKUP

Check Your Facts

1 Why is it important to wash your hands often?

2 CRITICAL THINKING Think about what oil does for your skin. What do you think might happen if you used harsh soap or bathed too often?

3 List three ways to protect your skin from the sun.

Set Health Goals

4 Think back over the past two days. How many times did you go outside, and how long did you stay out each time? Write down the different ways you protected yourself from the sun. Then think of ways you could do even better next time. Write these ideas down too.

Caring for My Teeth and Gums

Some of your adult teeth may grow in this year. You will need them for biting, chewing, and even talking. These teeth will last for the rest of your life if you take good care of them.

What can cause problems with teeth and gums?

Plaque (PLAK) is a sticky coating that is always forming on teeth. Plaque has bacteria that break down bits of food and give off acids. These acids can make a hole called a **cavity** (KA•vuh•tee) in a tooth.

Look at the diagram below. A cavity can grow through the enamel, into the dentin, and even into the pulp. A deep cavity can even kill the tooth.

When plaque stays on a tooth and hardens, it can make the gum weak. If the gum gets very weak, teeth may fall out.

▼ You can protect your teeth by flossing and brushing away plaque. Chewing a *disclosing tablet* makes areas with plaque dark red.

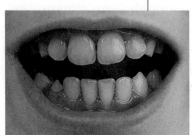

The Parts of a Tooth

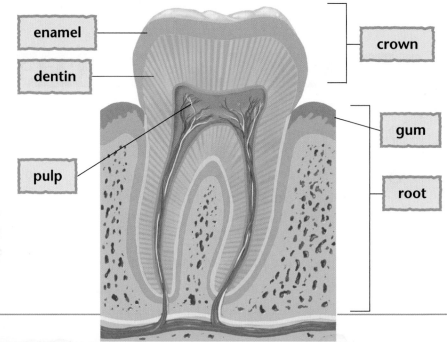

enamel

dentin

crown

gum

pulp

root

How can I floss my teeth?

Plaque can build up on all the surfaces of your teeth. It can also build up between your teeth. To remove plaque from between your teeth, you need a special thread called **dental floss**. Using this thread is called flossing.

▲ Plan to floss once a day. It's a good idea to floss just before you brush your teeth.

Look at the pictures to see how to floss. Break off about 18 inches of dental floss. Wrap one end of it around the middle finger of one hand. Guide the floss with your thumbs and index fingers. Push the floss gently between two teeth. Rub gently back and forth as you move the floss toward the gum. Also rub near the gum line of one tooth and then the other. Remove the floss. Unwind it a bit to reach a clean part. Repeat for each tooth.

How can I brush my teeth?

Brushing gets rid of plaque on the front, back, and top of each tooth. Use a toothbrush with soft bristles. Soft bristles will clean your teeth without hurting your gums. Use a toothpaste that has **fluoride** (FLAWR•yd). Fluoride is a chemical that makes teeth stronger and harder. Strong, hard teeth are less likely to get cavities.

Look at the pictures to see how to brush. Brush with short, tooth-wide back and forth movements on all your teeth. Brush along the gum line too. Spend extra time on your back teeth. They have deep pits where plaque can collect. Turn your toothbrush to reach the inner sides of your front teeth. When you finish brushing, spit out the toothpaste. Rinse your mouth with water.

JOURNAL

Keep a record of how you care for your teeth and gums every day for a week. Then look over your journal to make sure you're taking good care of your teeth and gums.

Activity **Practice Flossing and Brushing** Look carefully at the pictures on pages 75 and 76. With a partner, take turns acting out how to floss and brush your teeth. Explain each step as you act it out.

▶ Brush your teeth at least twice a day, once in the morning and again at night.

How can I protect my teeth from injury?

Your teeth are very strong and hard. But if you use them for cutting or tearing things other than food, you can harm the tooth enamel. For example, you should never open food packages with your teeth.

If you play sports, wear a mouth guard to protect your teeth from being hit or injured in a fall. A mouth guard is made of plastic. You can buy one at a store, or a dentist can make one for you.

If a tooth gets knocked out, put it back in place. If it is dirty, lightly rinse it first in a little milk or water. Hold it, and go right to the dentist. The dentist may be able to save the tooth.

LIFE SKILLS FOCUS

Make Decisions

Alan plays roller hockey. His coach recommends that all players wear mouth guards, but his friends say they aren't going to wear them. Use the decision-making steps shown on page *ix* to help Alan decide what to do.

• • •

◄ Dentists recommend mouth guards for football, baseball, basketball, hockey, and soccer players.

LESSON CHECKUP

Check Your Facts

❶ CRITICAL THINKING **How do you help your gums when you remove plaque from your teeth?**

❷ **When should you floss your teeth? When should you brush?**

❸ **What kind of toothbrush and toothpaste should you use? Why?**

Use Life Skills

❹ MAKE DECISIONS **Make a list of your favorite activities. Circle the activities you need a mouth guard for. Make up your own list of rules to help you decide when to use your mouth guard.**

MAIN IDEA
Caring for your ears and nose helps you stay healthy.

WHY LEARN THIS? Learning about your ears and nose will help you take good care of them.

VOCABULARY
• ear canal
• eardrum

Caring for My Ears and Nose

You go for a walk after it rains. You hear splashes as you walk through a puddle. Everything smells clean and damp. Your ears and nose help you enjoy the things around you, so take good care of them.

What can cause problems with hearing?

Your ear has three main parts—the outer ear, the middle ear, and the inner ear. The diagram below shows the three parts. Sound enters your ear through your **ear canal**. This is part of your outer ear. The opening you can see in your ear is the beginning of your ear canal.

▶ The part of the ear you can see collects sound waves and channels them into your ear canal.

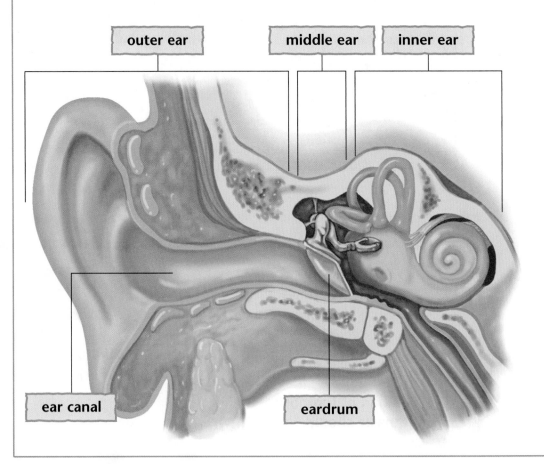

outer ear middle ear inner ear

ear canal

eardrum

Noise can hurt!

Your **eardrum** is at the other end of your ear canal. Sound waves make the eardrum move back and forth. This movement sends the waves on to the inner ear. The inner ear turns the waves into nerve signals. These signals travel to your brain, and you hear a sound.

Some things can harm your ears. Bacteria in your ear can give you an ear infection. An ear infection can make your ear hurt. You may also have trouble hearing. If this happens, tell an adult. The adult may take you to a doctor. The doctor may give you medicine to help your ear heal.

Loud sounds also can harm your ears. Over time such sounds can cause you to have trouble hearing. Loud music, loud machines, and loud traffic all can cause hearing problems. You may not notice these problems for many years. By then it will be too late to correct the harm to your ears.

▲ Noise from these things can cause hearing problems over time. What are some other sounds that might harm your hearing?

How can I take care of my ears?

Write a Story

On Your Own Think about ways to keep your ears safe. Think about things you should and should not do. Write a story about what you can do to have a safe hearing day.

You cannot stop all the things that might hurt your hearing, but you can avoid most of them. Stay away from noisy places. Turn the sound down when you listen to the TV, radio, or CD player. Also keep the sound low when you play video games. When you use headphones, you should still be able to hear sounds around you. If you can't, you may be hurting your ears.

Getting hit on your ears also can hurt your hearing. Wear a helmet when you play rough sports. This will help protect your ears.

You can wash the outsides of your ears with a washcloth. But do not stick anything into the ear canal. Doing this can poke a hole in the eardrum and damage hearing.

◀ Wearing a helmet will help protect your ears when you play hockey, baseball, or football.

How can I protect my nose?

Have you ever had a hard bump to your nose? If you have, you know how much it can hurt. Injuries to the nose usually heal quickly. Still, you need to take care of your nose to feel your best.

Taking care of your nose is especially important when you have a cold. Always blow your nose gently. Keep both nostrils and your mouth open. If you blow your nose too hard, you can send bacteria from your throat through a tiny tube into your middle ear. This can give you an earache.

Blowing your nose too hard also can break blood vessels. When that happens, your nose may bleed. If you get a nosebleed, stand or sit up and lean forward. Gently pinch your nose. Breathe through your mouth. The bleeding should stop soon.

▶ **If bleeding from your nose doesn't stop after a short time, visit your doctor for help.**

HUMAN BODY CONNECTION

The Sense Organs

When your nose feels stuffed up, what happens to your senses of smell and taste? Turn to pages 2 and 3 of The Amazing Human Body to learn more about the nose and your senses.

● ● ●

LESSON CHECKUP

Check Your Facts

❶ Explain how your eardrum helps you hear.

❷ What can happen if you listen to loud sounds over a period of years?

❸ CRITICAL THINKING Why might spicy foods taste good to you when you have a cold?

❹ What should you do if you get a nosebleed?

Set Health Goals

❺ Make a list of common noises that could hurt your hearing over time. Next to each noise, write one or more ways you could protect your ears from that noise. Share your list with your family. Make plans to put your ideas into action.

Exercise and Rest for Fun and Health

You come in from playing outside. You are laughing and have lots of energy. In fact, you feel great. That's because you have good physical fitness.

How can I exercise for fitness?

Exercise helps you become and stay physically fit. **Exercise** (EK•ser•syz) is any activity that makes your body work hard. Running games and sports are exercise. Swimming is exercise. Jumping rope is exercise. Riding a bike is exercise. Even walking is exercise.

Different kinds of exercise help your body in different ways. Some exercises make your muscles strong. For example, bicycling uphill strengthens your leg muscles. Some exercises stretch your muscles. Doing gymnastics stretches your arm, leg, and back muscles.

Aerobic exercises (air•OH•bik EK•ser•sy•zuhs) strengthen your heart and lungs by making them work harder.

Activity **Choose Exercises** Look at the exercises in the pictures. Which ones do you already like to do? Which ones would you like to try? Tell which exercises you will do this week to be fit.

Aerobic exercise helps your whole body work better. The activities in the pictures can be aerobic exercises. They are aerobic if you do them hard enough to speed up your heart and breathing rates. But you should not exercise so hard that you can't talk with a friend. Also, you must exercise for at least twenty minutes.

You can exercise by yourself or with friends or family. Exercise can be fun. It can cheer you up if you feel angry, sad, or stressed.

◀ There are many different kinds of aerobic exercise. Try to do aerobic exercise at least three times each week.

How do rest and sleep help me stay fit?

Exercise is good for your body. Rest is also good for you. After exercise your body needs to rest. When you rest, you breathe more slowly. Your heart beats more slowly too. Your muscles have a chance to relax. After resting, you may have more energy. You may want to do something active again.

Sleep is an important way to rest. When you sleep, your whole body slows down. Your senses become dull. You breathe slowly and deeply. Your heart beats slowly. Your muscles relax. Your body repairs itself during sleep. It makes new blood cells and bone cells.

Sleep gives your brain a chance to rest too. If you do not sleep much one night, you may have trouble thinking the next day. You may have a hard time remembering things. Extra sleep the next night will help you think better and feel better.

Did you know?

You dream for several hours every night. When you dream, your eyes dart back and forth. Your eyelids may flutter. But your arms and legs probably don't move much at all.

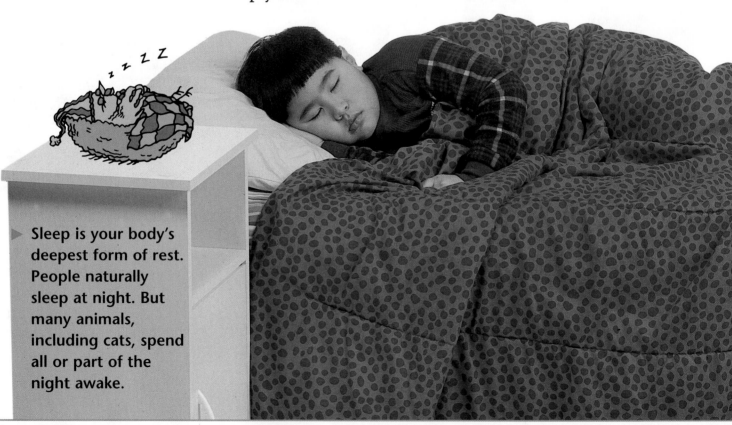

Sleep is your body's deepest form of rest. People naturally sleep at night. But many animals, including cats, spend all or part of the night awake.

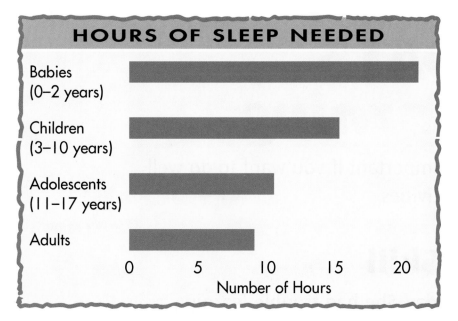

HOURS OF SLEEP NEEDED

Babies
(0–2 years)

Children
(3–10 years)

Adolescents
(11–17 years)

Adults

| 0 | 5 | 10 | 15 | 20 |

Number of Hours

▲ At different ages, people need different amounts of sleep. How much sleep do you need to feel your best?

As you grow, the amount of sleep you need changes. Right now you need ten to fourteen hours of sleep every night to stay healthy. Babies need more sleep than you do. Most adults need less.

LIFE SKILLS FOCUS

Make Decisions

Amber's friends want to play computer games on Saturday. Amber likes to be with her friends, but she also wants to get some exercise. Use the decision-making steps shown on page *ix* to help Amber satisfy both needs.

• • •

LESSON CHECKUP

Check Your Facts

❶ What are two ways exercise can help your body?

❷ CRITICAL THINKING Of the exercises you do, which are aerobic exercises?

❸ CRITICAL THINKING Why do you think babies need so much more sleep than adults do?

❹ Why is sleep important?

Use Life Skills

❺ REFUSE Imagine that you are spending the night at a friend's home. Your friend wants you to stay up late and play games. You know you need your sleep. Write down three ways you could politely say *no* to your friend.

SET GOALS
for Learning

Getting enough rest is important if you want to do well in school and other activities.

Learn This Skill

Lisa was very sleepy today. She had trouble learning. She could not pay attention and had trouble sitting still and listening.

1. Set a goal.

Lisa wanted to feel more awake in class.

2. Plan steps to help you meet the goal.

Lisa's dad suggested she go to bed earlier so she could get the rest she needed.

3. Monitor progress toward the goal.

Lisa and her dad made a chart she could fill in. Each night she went to bed on time, she gave herself a star.

4. Evaluate the goal.

When Lisa got the sleep she needed, she felt better at school. She could pay attention in class.

Practice This Skill

Use the steps to help you solve the problems.

Steps for Setting Goals

1. Set a goal.
2. Plan steps to help you meet the goal.
3. Monitor progress toward the goal.
4. Evaluate the goal.

A. Gene wants to spend more time reading. Use the goal-setting steps to help Gene find time to read.

B. Carrie wants to exercise at least three times each week. Use the goal-setting steps to help her.

MAIN IDEA
Exercising safely means following some simple safety rules.

WHY LEARN THIS? Most injuries can be prevented. But if you are injured, you should know what to do.

VOCABULARY
• warm-up
• cool-down

▶ Doing a warm-up before hard exercise and a cool-down afterward can help keep you from getting hurt. Both your warm-up and your cool-down should include stretching activities.

Staying Safe While Exercising

You are playing soccer with your friends. One by one your friends stop playing. One has a bruised shin. Another has a pulled muscle. One is thirsty and has a headache. The game would still be going on if everyone had followed simple safety rules.

How can I exercise safely?

Putting on safety gear before you start exercising is important. Soccer players should protect their legs with shin guards. They also need special shoes and mouth guards. Look through this chapter for pictures of different kinds of safety gear.

Warm up!

Warming up your muscles gets them ready for hard exercise. During your **warm-up**, stretch and do slow exercises for about five minutes. This helps prevent pulled muscles. After hard exercise, do slow exercise and stretching again. This is called a **cool-down**. A five minute cool-down helps prevent muscle soreness later.

Your body loses a lot of water during exercise. You see this when you sweat. Drinking water before, during, and after exercise can help prevent discomfort and illness.

▲ During exercise you can take small sips of water. This will cool you and replace some of the water you lose.

Work out!

Cool down!

What should I do if I get injured while exercising?

A little muscle soreness is normal after certain exercises. However, if you feel more than a mild soreness when you exercise, tell an adult. The adult will probably tell you to stop exercising for a while. You can see how you feel the next day. If you still feel sore, you can try a different exercise. Or you can do light exercise to give your muscles a chance to recover.

If you feel pain while exercising, you may have an injury. Stop right away. Tell an adult. The adult may give you an ice pack to keep the injury from swelling. Hold the ice on the injured spot for about fifteen minutes two or three times a day.

If you have a serious injury, the adult may take you to the doctor. The doctor may give you medicine or put a bandage or cast on the injured area. The doctor may decide you need extra help to heal. If so, he or she will send you to a physical therapist. A physical therapist helps people regain movement and strength so they can become active again soon.

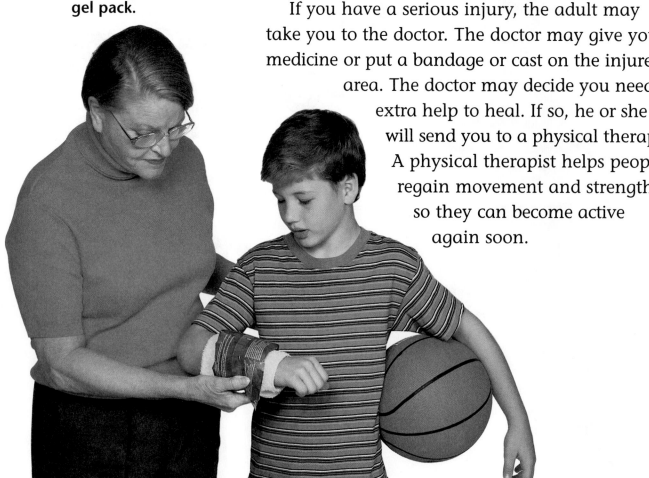

▼ If you put ice on an injury, wrap the ice in a towel or other cloth so it will not freeze your skin. The picture shows a reusable frozen gel pack.

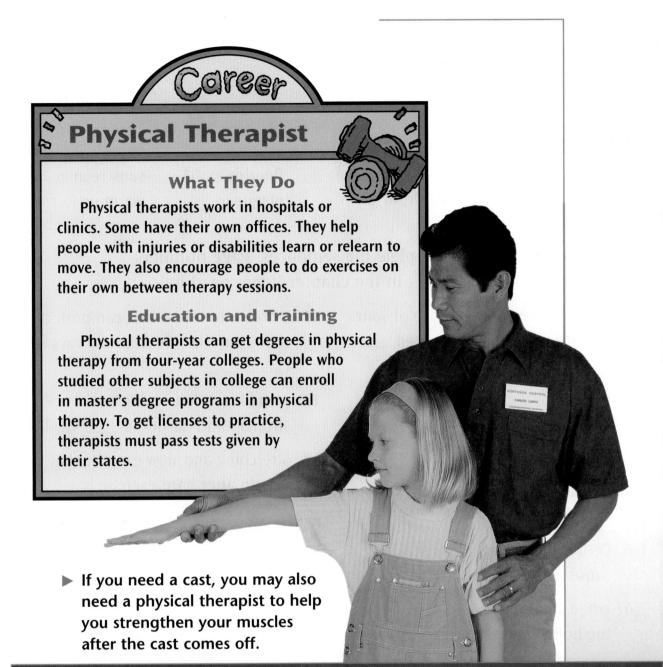

Career

Physical Therapist

What They Do

Physical therapists work in hospitals or clinics. Some have their own offices. They help people with injuries or disabilities learn or relearn to move. They also encourage people to do exercises on their own between therapy sessions.

Education and Training

Physical therapists can get degrees in physical therapy from four-year colleges. People who studied other subjects in college can enroll in master's degree programs in physical therapy. To get licenses to practice, therapists must pass tests given by their states.

► If you need a cast, you may also need a physical therapist to help you strengthen your muscles after the cast comes off.

LESSON CHECKUP

Check Your Facts

❶ CRITICAL THINKING List the safety gear for your favorite sport. Tell how each item helps keep players safe.

❷ Why is it important to do a warm-up and a cool-down when exercising?

❸ Why is it important to drink water before, during, and after exercising?

❹ CRITICAL THINKING You fall while jumping rope. Your ankle hurts. What should you do?

Set Health Goals

❺ Plan a weekly exercise program. Write which activity or activities you will do for aerobic exercise. Describe the warm-up and cool-down you will do during each exercise session. Try your plan for a week. Then write how you could make it better.

USE VOCABULARY

aerobic exercises (p. 82)   dental floss (p. 75)   exercise (p. 82)   pores (p. 70)

bacteria (p. 70)   ear canal (p. 78)   fluoride (p. 76)   sunscreen (p. 73)

cavity (p. 74)   eardrum (p. 79)   plaque (p. 74)   warm-up (p. 89)

cool-down (p. 89)

Use the terms above to complete the sentences. Page numbers in ( ) tell you where to look in the chapter if you need help.

1. Sweat comes to the surface of your skin through tiny holes called ____.

2. The sticky coating that forms on your teeth is called ____.

3. The opening that you can see in your ear is the beginning of your ____.

4. Any activity that makes your body work hard is ____.

5. Certain tiny living things that may cause illness are called ____.

6. When acids make a hole in a tooth, the hole is called ____.

7. The part that moves back and forth at the end of the ear canal is the ____.

8. Exercises that strengthen your heart and lungs by making them work harder are called ____.

9. The special thread you use to remove plaque between teeth is ____.

10. Stretching and slow exercise that you do before hard exercise is a ____.

11. A cream or lotion that can protect skin from the sun's harmful rays is called ____.

12. A chemical that makes teeth stronger and harder is ____.

13. Stretching and slow exercise that you do after hard exercise is a ____.

CHECK YOUR FACTS

Page numbers in ( ) tell you where to look if you need help.

14. Describe the correct way to brush your teeth. (p. 76)

15. Tell two things you can do to exercise safely. (pp. 88–89)

16. List three ways to take good care of your ears and prevent hearing problems. (p. 80)

17. Explain why you need to protect your skin from the sun. (p. 72)

18. Use the bar graph to tell the greatest number of hours of sleep needed by people in each age group. (p. 85)

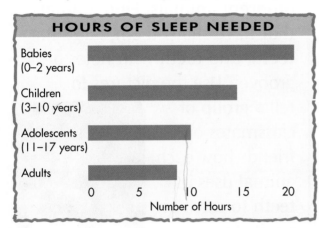

HOURS OF SLEEP NEEDED

	Number of Hours
Babies (0–2 years)	
Children (3–10 years)	
Adolescents (11–17 years)	
Adults	

21. **Manage Stress** Imagine that you are feeling stressed or angry about something that happened at school. What could you do for half an hour when you get home that would help you feel happier and build your fitness? Give details.

22. **Make Decisions** Imagine that you are spending the night at a friend's house. When you unload your backpack, you realize that you forgot your toothbrush. Decide what you would do. Tell how you made your decision.

THINK CRITICALLY

19. Why might someone who seldom washes his or her hands be likely to get or spread a cold?

20. Would it be a good idea to clean the inside of your ears with cotton swabs? Explain.

Promote Health **Home and Community**

1. Talk to family members about what you have learned in this chapter. Together, make a plan for taking care of yourselves. For example, you might go to the store together to choose a good sunscreen or toothpaste. Or you might come up with a family exercise program that everyone can enjoy.

2. Make posters about exercise safety. Get permission to display them at places in your community where people play sports or do other kinds of exercise.

Activities

Teeth of Different Sorts

With a Partner • Look for pictures that show the teeth of different animals. Find animals that have sharp teeth, large flat teeth, and teeth with holes or grooves. Use the pictures to tell a group of classmates or friends how each animal uses its teeth to catch or eat its food.

Warm-up and Cool-down Collage

With a Team • Brainstorm good ways to warm up before and cool down after different kinds of hard exercise. A warm-up and a cool-down should use the same muscles that the hard exercise does. Make a collage using pictures of the exercises you brainstormed.

Sleepy Time

On Your Own • Keep track of your sleep for a week. Write down the time you go to sleep each night and the time you wake up each morning. Make a bar graph that shows how long you slept each night.

The Nose Knows

At Home • Ask an adult to help you gather some "mystery foods" for family members to sample. Have those family members put on blindfolds, hold their noses, and try to identify the foods by taste. Then have them try to identify the foods without holding their noses. Talk about how the nose affects taste as well as smell.

Multiple Choice

Choose the letter of the correct answer.

1. What should you do before you eat?
   a. apply sunscreen b. bathe
   c. wash hands   d. floss

2. Brushing gets rid of ____.
   a. minerals   b. plaque
   c. cavities   d. fluoride

3. Avoiding loud sounds is one way to protect your sense of ____.
   a. hearing   b. smell
   c. sight   d. taste

4. Bicycling uphill ____ leg muscles.
   a. speeds up   b. stretches
   c. strengthens   d. slows down

5. If you get hurt while exercising, ____ is the best thing to help stop the swelling.
   a. hot water   b. bandages
   c. cold water   d. ice

Modified True or False

Write *true* or *false*. If a sentence is false, replace the underlined term to make the sentence true.

6. Washing with soap is <u>a poor way</u> to get rid of bacteria on your hands.

7. One way to protect uncovered skin from the sun is to put <u>sunscreen</u> on.

8. Remove plaque from between teeth by <u>rinsing your mouth</u>.

9. Baseball players should wear <u>mouth guards</u> to protect their ears.

10. Blowing your nose too hard can give you an <u>earache</u>.

11. You should do aerobic exercise for <u>at least twenty minutes</u> at a time.

12. People your age need <u>seven to nine hours</u> of sleep each night to stay healthy.

13. Drinking <u>water</u> before, during, and after exercising can help prevent discomfort and illness.

Short Answer

Write a complete sentence to answer each question.

14. How can the sun harm you?

15. Tell what to do if a tooth is knocked out.

16. How can you protect your hearing when listening to music at home?

17. Tell what to do to stop a nosebleed.

18. When you exercise, how should you warm up and cool down?

Writing in Health

Write paragraphs to answer each item.

19. Describe a perfect "healthful habits day."

20. Someone doesn't want to exercise because it's "boring." Tell how you would change his or her mind.

CHAPTER 4

Food for a Healthy Body

MAKE A FOOD DISPLAY

As you work through this chapter, think about which foods you need to eat to stay healthy. Cut out pictures from magazines and food labels, and arrange them on paper plates. Include information about each food, and explain why it is healthful. Put your food display in the school cafeteria.

For other activities, visit the Harcourt Learning Site. www.harcourtschool.com

Why My Body Needs Food

MAIN IDEA
Eating healthful foods from plants and animals is important to good health.

WHY LEARN THIS? In order to eat a healthful diet, you need to understand which foods are good for you.

VOCABULARY
• nutrients
• nutrition
• diet
• fiber

When you eat, does it matter whether you eat bananas or potato chips? Yogurt or french fries? Carrots or cookies? You bet it does! Some foods are more healthful than others. Eating healthful foods is important in keeping your body healthy.

Why is food important?

You cannot live without food. Food gives your body energy. You need energy to grow. You need energy to be active. You need energy to read, write, and think. You even need energy to sleep!

Nutrients (NOO•tree•uhnts) are the parts of food that help your body grow and get energy. There are many different kinds of nutrients. You get all the nutrients you need by eating different kinds of foods.

Nutrition (nu•TRIH•shuhn) is the study of food and how it affects the body. Knowing about nutrition can help you stay healthy.

◀ What are some ways people use energy? ▼

These foods help you grow.

These foods give you energy and help you grow.

These foods help your body work as it should.

Why should you eat different kinds of foods?

Loni eats leftover pizza for breakfast. Ali snacks on popcorn and pretzels. Cathy often has rice and vegetables for dinner. The foods a person usually eats and drinks make up his or her **diet** (DY•uht). What foods are a part of your diet?

Some diets are more healthful than others. For you to stay healthy, your diet must give your body all the nutrients it needs. Your diet also must include **fiber**, the woody part of plants. Fiber helps keep you healthy. Many fruits and vegetables contain fiber. Grains, such as brown rice, and foods made from grains, such as oatmeal and bread, also contain fiber.

Variety is important in a diet. Some foods give your body energy. Some foods help you grow. Other foods help parts of your body work well. The photograph shows some healthful foods that do these jobs. Which of these foods do you eat?

HUMAN BODY CONNECTION

The Intestines

Fiber helps keep food moving through your small and large intestines. Look at the digestive system on page 8 at the front of the book. Trace the intestines from one end to the other.

● ● ●

▲ Wheat is needed to make bread. Wheat is a grain that is harvested in mid- or late summer.

▲ The wheat is taken to a factory to be ground into a fine powder called flour.

Where does food come from?

Many of the foods we eat come from plants. Fruits and vegetables come from plants. So do beans, nuts, and seeds. Grains used to make cereals and breads also come from plants. Some common grains are corn, wheat, oats, and rice. Look at the pictures to see how bread is made.

When plant crops are ripe, they are harvested. Some plant foods are sold fresh. Others are sent to factories where they are canned, packaged, or frozen.

Career

Farm Operator

What They Do

Farm operators raise grains, fruits, vegetables, livestock, and dairy cows. They plan, plant, and care for crops. They care for animals. They harvest crops and send foods to market.

Education and Training

Many farm operators grow up on farms. Farm operators need strong science and math skills. Some may use computers. People without farming experience can go to college to learn how to grow crops or raise animals.

▲ At large bakeries wheat flour is made into loaves of bread. The loaves are packaged in plastic bags.

▲ Trucks bring loaves of fresh bread to grocery stores every day.

Most of the other foods people eat come from animals. We eat meat from cows, sheep, pigs, chicken, and fish. Most of the eggs we eat come from chickens. Most of the milk we drink comes from cows. After the cows are milked, the milk is heated to make it safe to drink. Then it is put into containers. Some milk is made into cheeses, butter, ice cream, or yogurt.

All kinds of plant and animal foods come from farms across the United States. Some foods even come from other countries. When ready for sale, fresh and prepared foods are sent to markets. They may be sent by truck or train. Inside the market, food is placed on shelves or in cold storage. Finally, it ends up on your table.

LESSON CHECKUP

Check Your Facts

1 Why are nutrients important to good health?

2 What is nutrition?

3 Where does food come from?

4 Describe how wheat becomes the bread you eat.

Set Health Goals

5 What kinds of foods make up your diet? List the foods you eat often. Tell which are plant foods and which are animal foods. What can you do to make your diet more healthful?

The Food Guide Pyramid and Healthful Meals

The Cortéz family wants to be healthy. Every Sunday they sit down and plan their meals for the week. They plan for three meals and two snacks each day. The family chooses a variety of foods. They want to make sure everyone gets all the nutrients he or she needs.

What makes a meal healthful?

By itself a potato is not a healthful meal. But if you eat it with salad, chicken, and a glass of milk, you will have a healthful meal. A healthful meal includes a variety of foods. Eating a variety of foods gives your body the nutrients it needs.

The **Food Guide Pyramid** (FOOD GYD PIR•uh•mid) is a tool to help you choose foods for a healthful diet. It has six groups. The Food Guide Pyramid tells how many servings you should eat from each group each day. A **serving** is the measured amount of a food you would probably eat during a meal or as a snack.

The bread group is the largest group in the Food Guide Pyramid. It includes bread, pasta, rice, and cereal. The smallest section of the pyramid is the fats, oils, and sweets group. You don't need to eat many of these foods.

Fruits are one group. Vegetables are another. Milk products make up a group. Meat, fish, poultry, eggs, nuts, and dried beans make up another group.

Fats, oils, and sweets group Eat very little from this group each day.

Meat, poultry, fish, dry beans, eggs, and nuts group Eat 2–3 servings from this group each day.

Milk, yogurt, and cheese group Eat 2–3 servings a day.

Fruit group Eat 2–4 servings each day.

Vegetable group Eat 3–5 servings each day.

Bread, cereal, rice, and pasta group Eat 6–11 servings from this group each day.

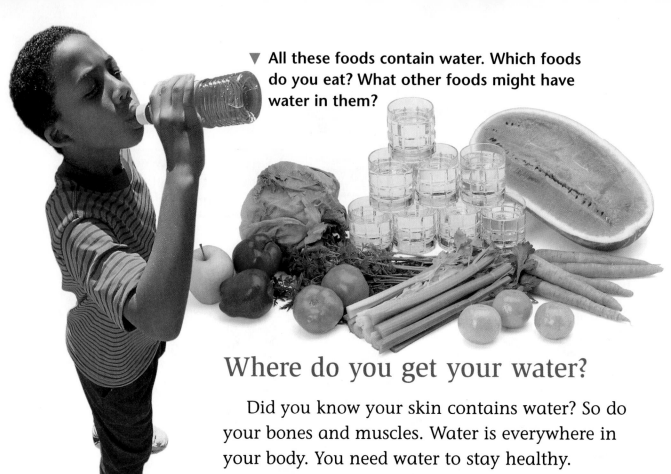

▼ All these foods contain water. Which foods do you eat? What other foods might have water in them?

Where do you get your water?

Did you know your skin contains water? So do your bones and muscles. Water is everywhere in your body. You need water to stay healthy.

You get some water from the foods you eat. Fruits such as apples, peaches, and melons contain water. Vegetables such as lettuce and carrots also have water. But to get enough water, you need to drink six to eight glasses of water each day.

Fluoride (FLAWR•yd) is a nutrient your body needs in small amounts. It helps keep your teeth healthy. Fluoride is often added to the water that is piped to homes. If you get your water from a water company, you may get some of this fluoride each time you drink water from your faucet.

Some people don't drink water that is piped to their homes. They buy bottled water to drink or get their water from a well.

Sometimes fluoride and other chemicals are removed from bottled water. People who drink water without fluoride, such as bottled water or water from private wells, may need to get fluoride in other ways. Sometimes they get fluoride treatments from a dentist.

104

Why eat three meals a day?

Everything you do uses energy. Even when you are not doing anything, your body is using energy. Your body needs energy all day.

Different activities use different amounts of energy. When you ride your bike, your body uses a lot of energy. When you sit and read, it uses less.

All the energy your body uses comes from the food you eat. Your body uses energy throughout the day. The Food Guide Pyramid can help you eat foods to provide your energy needs. If you use the guide to eat foods from each food group every day, you will have a **balanced diet** (BA•luhnst DY•uht).

Suppose you ate all the foods you need each day at one meal. Your body could not use all that food at once. It's important to eat meals throughout the day. Spacing meals gives your body the energy and nutrients it needs all day.

LIFE SKILLS FOCUS

Make Decisions
Kim is always late. She often skips breakfast so she won't miss the bus. This makes Kim tired and cranky. Use the steps for making decisions on page *ix* to help Kim get the energy she needs and still catch the bus.

▶ **What provided these boys with the energy they need to play their favorite sport?**

LESSON CHECKUP

Check Your Facts

1. What is the Food Guide Pyramid?
2. What are the food groups in the Food Guide Pyramid?
3. How can you make sure you get enough water?
4. CRITICAL THINKING How can you eat a balanced diet?

Set Health Goals

5. Think back over what you've eaten for lunch the last three days. Did you eat foods from every food group in the Food Guide Pyramid? How many things did you eat from each group? How can you make your lunches more healthful?

MAIN IDEA
Snacks are an important part of a healthful diet.

WHY LEARN THIS? You can use what you learn to help you choose healthful snacks.

VOCABULARY
• snacks

Healthful Snack Choices

Seth gets home from school every day at three o'clock. He heads straight for the refrigerator. He's starving! Milk, cheese, crackers, grapes, apples, carrots, celery. What will Seth choose today?

Like most children, Seth eats a few **snacks**—food between meals—every day. Snacks are a part of a healthful diet. They keep you from getting too hungry. They also give you the energy and nutrients you need. Snacks are especially important if you are active.

People eat snacks for many reasons. You might be hungry. You may eat snacks when you are with friends. You may want a snack when you are tired. You may have a snack to celebrate a happy time, such as a birthday.

A quick snack gives me energy!

What makes a snack healthful?

As you use the Food Guide Pyramid, remember to include snacks in your diet. Snacks help you get nutrients you may not get during meals. A plum or pear as a snack gives you a fruit serving. A granola bar or half a bagel gives you a serving from the bread, cereal, rice, and pasta group.

Some snacks are not healthful. They don't give you the nutrients you need most. Potato chips and chocolate bars are mostly fats and sweets. You should eat these foods only in small amounts.

Healthful snacks don't contain a lot of fats, oils, or sweets. Some healthful snacks are listed below.

This snack counts as a serving of fruit.

- fresh fruit
- raw vegetables
- whole grain cereal
- orange juice
- milk
- raisins
- lowfat yogurt
- unbuttered popcorn
- whole wheat crackers
- cheese
- peanut butter sandwich

Which foods in the healthful snacks list do you like? Remember these foods the next time you race for the kitchen. Find yourself a healthful snack!

LESSON CHECKUP

Check Your Facts
1. What is a snack?
2. CRITICAL THINKING What are two reasons snacks are important?
3. What are two unhealthful snacks?
4. Give four examples of healthful snacks.

Use Life Skills
5. COMMUNICATE Write a letter to an adult family member. Explain why you like to eat healthful snacks. Include suggestions for five healthful snacks that you would eat. Ask if you might help shop for these foods.

MAKE DECISIONS
About Snacks

Choosing snacks is something most people do every day.
This skill will help you make healthful choices.

Learn This Skill

Belinda has a skating lesson in thirty minutes. Her
friends are ready to go, but she wants to eat a healthful
snack that will give her energy during her lesson.

1. Find out about the choices you could make.

Belinda opens the refrigerator to check out her choices. What will she choose?

2. Imagine the possible result of each choice.

Belinda thinks about what would taste good. She also thinks about how long each snack will take to fix and eat.

3. Make what seems to be the best choice.

Belinda chooses an apple because it's her favorite fruit. It's also ready to eat!

4. Think about the result of your choice.

Belinda got a healthful snack and didn't keep her friends waiting.

Practice This Skill

Use this summary as you solve the problems below.

Steps for Making Decisions

1. Find out about the choices you could make.

2. Imagine the possible result of each choice.

3. Make what seems to be the best choice.

4. Think about the result of your choice.

A. Howard is bringing drinks for the baseball team. He may bring cola, fruit juice, or water. Use the steps to help Howard make his choice.

B. Ann is planning a snack for a hike. She needs a healthful snack she can carry easily. What are some possible choices? What is the best choice? Why?

Being a Wise Food Shopper

MAIN IDEA
Foods vary in their ingredients and prices.

WHY LEARN THIS? You can use what you learn to make wise choices when shopping for food.

VOCABULARY
• ingredients
• food label

Sabrena and her father go shopping together every week. By shopping together, they each get a variety of foods they like. As they shop, Sabrena and her father carefully look at all the labels. They want to be sure the foods they buy are healthful.

How can you choose among food products?

Many foods are packaged. Packaged foods include cake mixes, canned fruits, and bread. These foods are made of more than one thing. The things that go into a food are its **ingredients** (in•GREE•dee•uhnts).

► There are so many different cereals! What do you think helped Sabrena and her father make their choice?

Activity **Compare Soups** Compare the ingredients in the canned and dried chicken noodle soup. See what is listed first and second in each food. How many ingredients does each have? Look for ingredients that are in both soups. Which soup do you think is more healthful? Why?

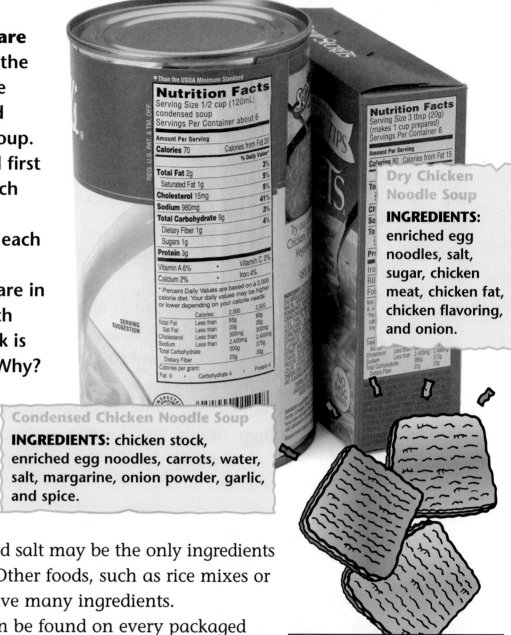

Nutrition Facts
Serving Size 1/2 cup (120mL)
condensed soup
Servings Per Container about 6

Amount Per Serving	
Calories 70	Calories from Fat 20
	% Daily Value*
Total Fat 2g	3%
Saturated Fat 1g	5%
Cholesterol 15mg	5%
Sodium 980mg	41%
Total Carbohydrate 9g	3%
Dietary Fiber 1g	4%
Sugars 1g	
Protein 3g	

Vitamin A 6%	•	Vitamin C 0%
Calcium 2%	•	Iron 4%

* Percent Daily Values are based on a 2,000 calorie diet. Your daily values may be higher or lower depending on your calorie needs:

		2,000	2,500
	Calories:	2,000	2,500
Total Fat	Less than	65g	80g
Sat Fat	Less than	20g	25g
Cholesterol	Less than	300mg	300mg
Sodium	Less than	2,400mg	2,400mg
Total Carbohydrate		300g	375g
Dietary Fiber		25g	30g

Calories per gram:
Fat 9 • Carbohydrate 4 • Protein 4

Nutrition Facts
Serving Size 3 tbsp (20g)
(makes 1 cup prepared)
Servings Per Container 6

Dry Chicken Noodle Soup

INGREDIENTS: enriched egg noodles, salt, sugar, chicken meat, chicken fat, chicken flavoring, and onion.

Condensed Chicken Noodle Soup

INGREDIENTS: chicken stock, enriched egg noodles, carrots, water, salt, margarine, onion powder, garlic, and spice.

Corn, water, and salt may be the only ingredients in a can of corn. Other foods, such as rice mixes or frozen dinners, have many ingredients.

A **food label** can be found on every packaged food. It gives information about how nutritious a food is. The information is called Nutrition Facts.

A food label also lists the ingredients in a food. You can use food labels to compare the ingredients in different foods. The ingredients are listed in order of amount. The first ingredient is the one used most in the food. The last ingredient is the one used least.

Food labels also show the amounts of different nutrients. Similar foods may have different nutrients. They may also have different amounts of each nutrient.

Nutrition Facts
Serving Size 16 Crackers
Servings per Container About 4

Amount per Serving	
Calories 140	Calories from Fat 50
	% Daily Value
Total Fat 6g	9%
Saturated Fat 1g	5%
Polyunsaturated Fat 0g	
Monounsaturated Fat 2g	
Cholesterol 0mg	0%
Sodium 180mg	8%
Total Carbohydrate 19g	6%
Dietary Fiber 2g	
Sugars 2g	
Protein 2g	

Vitamin A 0%	•	Vitamin C 0%
Calcium 2%	•	Iron 4%

Analyze Advertising and Media Messages
Some ads use "tricks" to get you to buy the product. Find an ad for a popular drink, such as juice or a sports drink. Use the steps on page *xv* to figure out what "tricks" are being used to help sell the drink.

▼ **Orange juice comes in many different packages.**

Why the price difference?

Kito and his brother need to buy orange juice. They can buy fresh juice, canned juice, or frozen juice. They can buy a big package or a small package. They can buy juice in cartons, cans, bottles, or boxes.

The boys want to get the best deal. But each package of juice has a different price. They are so confused!

One kind of food may have many different prices. Fresh foods are often most expensive. Frozen foods may cost more than canned foods.

Some foods cost more because they carry brand names. You know these names because you see them in ads. The ads cost a lot of money to make. But you help pay for the ads each time you buy the food.

A large supermarket may have its own store brand. You do not see many ads for these foods. So store brand foods are usually cheaper than brand-name foods.

Foods are sold in different amounts. A small can of juice costs less than a large can. But be careful. The juice in the small can may really be more expensive! You must compare the cost by weight or unit. The cost per ounce of the small can is probably higher than that of the large can. You can often find the unit cost on tags near the food on the store shelf.

Sometimes foods are packaged together. You can buy packages of boxed juice. Each box is a single serving. This type of package is expensive. You can save money by buying the juice in larger packages and using a clean, tightly closed jar to carry it in your lunch.

Compare Prices

On Your Own Compare peanut butter prices in the grocery store. Look at the sizes and prices. Look for tags on the shelf that tell you the price per unit. Read the ingredients labels. Which one would you buy? Why?

LESSON CHECKUP

Check Your Facts

❶ What are ingredients?

❷ How are food labels useful?

❸ What are three things that can affect the cost of food?

❹ CRITICAL THINKING Why do you have to be careful when comparing the prices of small and large packages?

Use Life Skills

❺ RESOLVE CONFLICTS Tess wants the small boxes of orange juice. Her sister wants to buy the frozen juice. Why might Tess want the small boxes? Why do you think her sister wants the frozen juice? How might they resolve their conflict?

Handling Food Safely

MAIN IDEA
Foods need to be stored and handled correctly to keep them safe to eat.

WHY LEARN THIS? You can use what you learn to stay well.

VOCABULARY
• spoiled
• pathogens

Jen is helping unload groceries. First, she quickly places the frozen foods in the freezer. Next, she puts the meat, chicken, and eggs in the refrigerator. She puts some of the fruits and vegetables in the refrigerator, too. Finally, Jen stacks the canned and dry foods in the cupboard.

Which foods need refrigerating?

Some foods spoil. A **spoiled** food is one that is unsafe to eat. Some foods spoil quickly. These foods usually need to be kept cold or frozen. You should store meat, milk, eggs, and leftovers in the refrigerator. This helps keep these foods from spoiling.

Foods such as meats, milk, and some fresh fruits and vegetables need to be refrigerated. Unopened canned foods do not.

Some foods need to go into the freezer. Already frozen foods, such as frozen vegetables, must stay frozen to be safe. Foods that are not bought frozen, such as meats, can be kept longer in the freezer.

What are some safety tips for preparing a meal?

Pathogens (PA•thuh•juhnz), or germs, in food can cause illness. If a food with pathogens touches another food, the pathogens can spread.

You can help keep pathogens from spreading. Before and after handling food, wash your hands with soap and warm water. Also wash and keep your work areas clean.

Meat and poultry can carry pathogens. You should not cut other foods on a surface that raw meat and poultry have touched. Cutting boards must be washed with soap and hot water.

Wrapping foods keeps out air and pathogens. It helps keep food safe. Always wrap foods before putting them away.

JOURNAL

Imagine you are preparing a picnic for your family. In your Health Journal make a list of foods you will bring. Then write how you will prepare and store the food safely.

▶ **Wrapping your food helps keep it fresh.**

LESSON CHECKUP

Check Your Facts
1. Why shouldn't you eat spoiled food?
2. Name four foods that must be kept in the refrigerator.
3. CRITICAL THINKING Why might you want to store meat in the freezer instead of the refrigerator?

Set Health Goals
4. When should you wash your hands throughout the day? When **do** you wash your hands? Set goals for keeping your hands cleaner. Try to meet your goals.

USE VOCABULARY

balanced diet (p. 105)	fluoride (p. 104)	ingredients (p. 110)	serving (p. 102)
diet (p. 99)	Food Guide Pyramid (p. 102)	nutrients (p. 98)	snacks (p. 106)
fiber (p. 99)	food label (p. 111)	nutrition (p. 98)	spoiled (p. 114)
		pathogens (p. 115)	

Use the terms above to complete the sentences. Page numbers in ( ) tell you where to look in the chapter if you need help.

1. The woody part of plants is ____.

2. Foods you eat between meals are ____.

3. The ____ is a tool to help you choose foods for a healthful diet.

4. A ____ gives you information about a food.

5. Parts of a food that help your body grow, get energy, and work well are ____.

6. When you have a ____, you eat foods from each food group every day.

7. The foods you usually eat or drink make up your ____.

8. A food that is unsafe to eat has ____.

9. ____ are the things that go into a food.

10. The study of food and how it affects the body is ____.

11. A ____ is the measured amount of a food you would probably eat during a meal or as a snack.

12. Germs in food that can cause illness are ____.

13. ____ is a nutrient that helps keep your teeth healthy.

CHECK YOUR FACTS

Page numbers in ( ) tell you where to look in the chapter if you need help.

14. What are some jobs of a farm operator? (p. 100)

15. How many glasses of water do you need each day? (p. 104)

16. How do snacks help you get the nutrients you need? (p. 107)

17. What does listing an ingredient first on a food label tell you about the ingredient? (p. 111)

Cholesterol	Less Than	300mg	300mg
Sodium	Less Than	2,400mg	2,400mg
Total Carbohydrate		300g	375g
Dietary Fiber		25g	30g

Calories per gram:
Fat 9 • Carbohydrate 4 • Protein 4

INGREDIENTS: Unbleached wheat flour, water, salt, yeast and soda.

18. Why is it important to wash your hands before eating? (p. 115)

THINK CRITICALLY

19. Name four plant foods and four animal foods.

20. What are three things you can do at home to help keep foods safe?

21. Make Decisions Imagine you are going to the movies with friends. They want to share hot buttered popcorn. You are trying to eat healthful snacks. Use the steps for making decisions to choose a more healthful snack you could have with your friends.

22. Make Decisions You go shopping with your parents. They want to buy the same kind of macaroni and cheese they usually get but they think the store brand, which comes in a larger box, is cheaper. How can you use the steps for making decisions to help your parents decide which product is a better buy?

Promote Health **Home and Community**

1. Sit down with your family to discuss what healthful snacks the whole family can enjoy. Make a shopping list that includes the snacks you agree on.
2. Talk with a farmer or a gardener who grows plants for food. Find out what kinds of things plants need to grow well. Share what you learn with your class.

Activities

Make Your Own Food Guide Pyramid

With a Team • Use boxes to make a model of a Food Guide Pyramid. Use pictures cut from food labels or magazines to show which foods belong in each part of the pyramid. Add labels to the pyramid that name each food group and tell how many servings a person should eat from the group each day.

Choosing Healthful Foods

On Your Own • Being safe in the kitchen is important for you and anyone else that might use the kitchen. Use pages 252–253 as a guide to make a kitchen safety checklist. You might want to place your checklist on the refrigerator so that everyone may use it.

cereal
pizza
popcorn
cheese
apple
animal crackers
corn

Local Foods

With a Partner • Find out what kinds of plant and animal foods are raised in your state. Draw a map of your state, and include pictures of the different types of foods.

Select Your Snacks

At Home • Look through your kitchen to see what kinds of snack foods are there. Make a list of the foods you find. Place a check beside each food you think makes a healthful snack.

Multiple Choice

Choose the letter of the correct answer.

1. ____ helps keep food moving through the digestive system.
   a. Nutrition   b. Fiber
   c. Fat   d. Cheese

2. Fluoride is a nutrient you may get from ____.
   a. juice   b. water
   c. fiber   d. vegetables

3. Snacks help you get the ____ you may not get during meals.
   a. nutrients   b. oils
   c. fats   d. nutrition

4. Your ____ is what you eat each day.
   a. serving   b. snack
   c. nutrition   d. diet

5. Foods such as ____ need to be refrigerated.
   a. canned fruit   b. chips
   c. meats   d. bread

Modified True or False

Write *true* or *false*. If a sentence is false, replace the underlined term to make the sentence true.

6. Nutrition is the study of <u>fiber</u> and how it affects the body.

7. Fruits and vegetables come from <u>animals</u>.

8. The <u>fruit</u> group is the largest group in the Food Guide Pyramid.

9. You need to drink extra <u>water</u> when you exercise.

10. You should eat fats and sweets in <u>large</u> amounts.

11. Fresh foods are usually <u>less</u> expensive than canned foods.

12. The first ingredient on a food label is the one used <u>least</u> in the food.

13. Some foods cost more because they carry <u>brand</u> names.

14. A spoiled food is <u>safe</u> to eat.

15. Wrapping foods helps keep <u>pathogens</u> from spreading.

Short Answer

Write a complete sentence to answer each question.

16. Why should you wash your hands before and after handling food?

17. How can you compare the costs of foods sold in different amounts?

18. Name two things on a food label.

19. Name three healthful snacks.

20. Name three foods that contain water.

21. Name a food that comes from animals.

22. List three common grains.

Writing in Health

Write paragraphs to answer each item.

23. Why should you eat a variety of foods?

24. Explain some safety tips for preparing a meal.

CHAPTER 5

Preventing Disease

Project

MAKE A GERM-FIGHTER BULLETIN BOARD Make a bulletin board with pictures that show things you can do to avoid spreading germs. Make your own drawings, and cut out or copy pictures from magazines and newspapers. For each picture, include a short sentence telling how the activity shown prevents the spread of germs.

For other activities, visit the Harcourt Learning Site. www.harcourtschool.com

What Is Disease?

Patty was not eating her favorite meal. "Don't you feel well?" her father asked. Patty said her head and throat hurt. Her father knew she was ill because of her symptoms. A **symptom** (SIMP•tuhm) is a sign that something is wrong in the body. A headache and sore throat are common symptoms of a cold or flu.

How do you feel when you are ill? Like Patty, you probably don't feel very well. An illness is a disease. A **disease** (dih•ZEEZ) is something that causes the body not to work normally.

There are many kinds of diseases. Some diseases spread from one person to another. Sneezing without covering your mouth is one way to spread diseases such as a cold or the flu. Some other diseases can't be spread to other people.

JOURNAL

In your Health Journal, describe how you felt the last time you had a cold or the flu. What were your symptoms? How long did you feel ill? Remember that your journal is private.

▼ You know you are ill if you have symptoms. Some common symptoms are fever, scratchy throat, coughing, headache, and body aches.

▶ People with disabilities might not be able to do some things. But there are many other things they *can* do.

How should you act toward people who are ill?

When friends have diseases that can spread, you should know how you can keep the disease from spreading to you. Different diseases spread in different ways.

Sometimes people have diseases or health problems that you cannot catch. Stacy has an illness that keeps her from walking. She uses a wheelchair to get around. Stacy's illness can't be spread to others, but it has caused her to have a disability. A disability is a physical or mental problem. You can't catch a disability.

People with illnesses and disabilities may feel bad because their bodies aren't working normally. You should treat people with diseases and disabilities the same way you treat your other friends. Imagine how you would feel if you were that person. Think about how an illness or a disability would affect you and how you would want to be treated.

LESSON CHECKUP

Check Your Facts

1 What is a disease?

2 How do you know if you have a disease?

3 CRITICAL THINKING Suppose a student in your class is home with a cold. Should you visit him? If not, what could you do instead?

Set Health Goals

4 Think about a time when you were ill. How did you feel? What made you feel better? List some ways to help a person with an illness feel better.

Some Diseases and Their Causes

A friend at school gets a cold. She sniffles and sneezes all day Monday. By Friday several people in your class are ill. A cold is an infectious disease. An **infectious disease** (in•FEK•shuhs dih•ZEEZ) is a disease that can spread from one person to another. Infectious diseases are caused by pathogens. **Pathogens** (PA•thuh•juhnz) are germs that cause disease. When your friend sneezed, she spread the pathogens that caused her disease to others.

What are some kinds of pathogens?

Two main kinds of pathogens cause infectious diseases. One kind is bacteria. **Bacteria** (bak•TIR•ee•uh) are very simple living things. They are each made of just one cell. They are so small that you can see them only with a microscope.

Activity **Find the Ways Pathogens Spread** How are these students spreading pathogens? List other ways that pathogens can be spread.

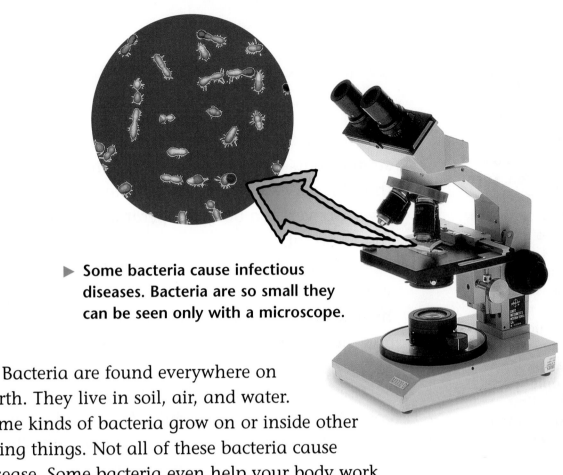

▶ Some bacteria cause infectious diseases. Bacteria are so small they can be seen only with a microscope.

Bacteria are found everywhere on Earth. They live in soil, air, and water. Some kinds of bacteria grow on or inside other living things. Not all of these bacteria cause disease. Some bacteria even help your body work normally.

However, a few kinds of bacteria *do* cause disease. When they get into your body, they can begin to multiply. They can grow into such large groups that your body cannot work normally. Then you become ill.

Another kind of pathogen is a virus. A **virus** (vy•ruhs) is one of the tiniest pathogens that cause disease. Viruses are even smaller than bacteria. Viruses must use cells in other living things to make more viruses. Viruses cause disease by destroying the cells they use.

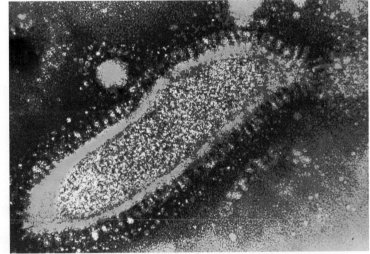

▲ Viruses also cause some infectious diseases. Viruses are even smaller than bacteria. Special microscopes must be used to see them. This virus has been magnified many hundreds of times.

Did you know?

Fall marks the start of cold and flu season. Even though cold, wet weather doesn't cause colds and influenza, these diseases are much more common in fall and winter. This may be because people spend more time inside, where viruses can spread more easily.

What are some infectious diseases?

One infectious disease that bacteria cause is strep throat. When you have strep throat, your throat is very sore and you may have a fever. A **fever** (FEE•ver) is a body temperature that is higher than normal.

Colds and flu are two kinds of infectious diseases viruses cause. When you have a cold, you may have a stuffy nose, a scratchy throat, and a cough. You may even have a fever. Colds usually last about a week.

The flu has many of the same symptoms as a cold. You also may have chills, fever, and body aches. The flu can make you feel very tired. The flu usually lasts one day to a week.

▼ If you have a very sore throat, your doctor may take a swab of your throat. The doctor will try to grow what's on the swab. If certain bacteria grow, you may have strep throat.

▲ When you have a cold or the flu, you need plenty of rest.

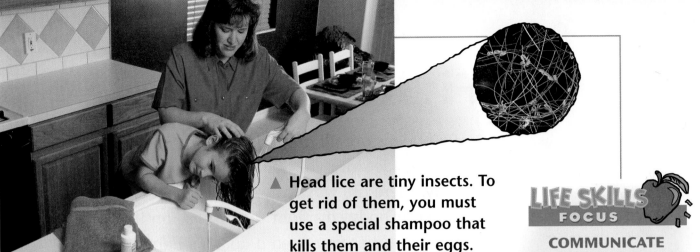

▲ Head lice are tiny insects. To get rid of them, you must use a special shampoo that kills them and their eggs.

LIFE SKILLS FOCUS

COMMUNICATE
Joyce is making a picture book to help a kindergarten class learn how infectious diseases spread. What should Joyce think about while she's planning her book? How can she communicate her message clearly? Use the steps for communicating shown on page *xii*.

What are other health problems that can spread?

Another common problem that can spread is head lice. People who have head lice can spread the lice by being near other people or by sharing things like combs, brushes, and hats.

Head lice are very small insects that crawl on skin and hair and feed on blood. As the lice feed, the head becomes very itchy. Other symptoms of head lice are tiny red bumps near the root of the hair on the head.

People who have head lice must use a special shampoo that kills the insects. The eggs in the hair must be removed with a fine comb or tweezers. All combs, brushes, clothing, and bed linens must be washed in very hot water to kill the lice and their eggs.

LESSON CHECKUP

Check Your Facts

❶ What are pathogens?

❷ How do pathogens cause infectious diseases?

❸ CRITICAL THINKING Is it a good idea to share a cup with a friend who doesn't seem ill? Why or why not?

Set Health Goals

❹ Think of a time when you caught an infectious disease from a friend or relative. How do you think you got the disease? Write down some things you might have done to keep from getting the disease.

Fighting Disease

MAIN IDEA
Most diseases can
be prevented and
treated.

**WHY LEARN
THIS?** You can use
what you learn to
help keep yourself
and others healthy.

VOCABULARY
• immune
• vaccine
• medicine

Pathogens are all around us. Sometimes
pathogens get into your body and cause disease.
Luckily, there are ways to treat most diseases.
Often your body can fight the disease on its
own. Sometimes you need a doctor's help.

How can you prevent disease?

Reggie wants Juan to come outside and play.
Juan's mom says that Juan has the flu. He can't
play with other children until he is well. She tells
Reggie that she doesn't want him to catch the flu
from Juan.

Staying away from people who are ill is only
one way to prevent disease. A very important
way to prevent disease is by washing your hands
with soap and water. Many objects that people
touch a lot, such as doorknobs and handrails, have
pathogens on them. Washing with soap and water
helps get rid of the pathogens on your hands.
Keeping your hands clean helps prevent disease.

▶ Reggie can't
play with Juan
because Juan
is ill. Learning
how diseases
are spread
helps you
know how to
stay healthy.

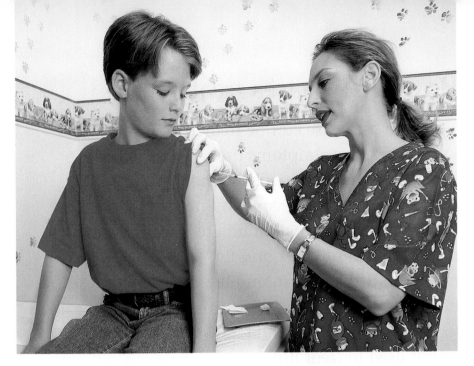

◀ A vaccine is usually given by injection. It will prevent one specific disease.

You can also prevent diseases by becoming immune to them. A person is **immune** (ih•MYOON) when a pathogen that causes a disease cannot make that person ill. People often become immune to a disease after they have had that disease. They also become immune when they get a vaccine for that disease. A **vaccine** (vak•SEEN) is a substance given to keep you from getting a certain kind of disease.

When you get a vaccine, a pathogen for a disease is put into your body. The pathogen has been weakened or killed so it can't make you ill. But it does cause your body to make a substance to fight the pathogen. If that pathogen gets in your body again, this substance will destroy it right away. You won't become ill.

When you are ill, you must also keep from spreading the disease to others. There are several easy things you can do. Wash your hands often. Cover your mouth and nose with a tissue when you cough or sneeze. Don't share anything that you have put in your mouth or near your nose. Doing these things will help keep others from catching your disease.

Some Diseases for Which There Are Vaccines

- Chicken pox
- Diphtheria
- Haemophilus Type B
- Hepatitis B
- Measles
- Mumps
- Pertussis
- Pneumonia
- Polio
- Rubella
- Tetanus

SCIENCE CONNECTION

Body Temperature

On Your Own How do you know when you have a fever? Find out what normal body temperature is. Then find out how high a body temperature must be to be a fever.

○ ○ ○

How are diseases treated?

Before a disease can be treated, you must know what the symptoms are. Always tell a parent, teacher, or caregiver when you feel ill. Then you will get the care you need.

Diseases are treated in different ways. Many diseases, such as colds and flu, are treated by resting in bed and drinking liquids. Sometimes diseases are treated with medicines. A **medicine** (MEH•duh•suhn) is a liquid, powder, cream, spray, or pill used to treat illness.

Not all medicines work alike. Some medicines kill the pathogen causing the disease. Medicines for strep throat and ear infections work like this. Other medicines treat the symptoms of a disease to make the person feel better. Cold medicines work like this. These medicines can help clear a stuffy nose and soothe a sore throat. But they cannot cure a cold.

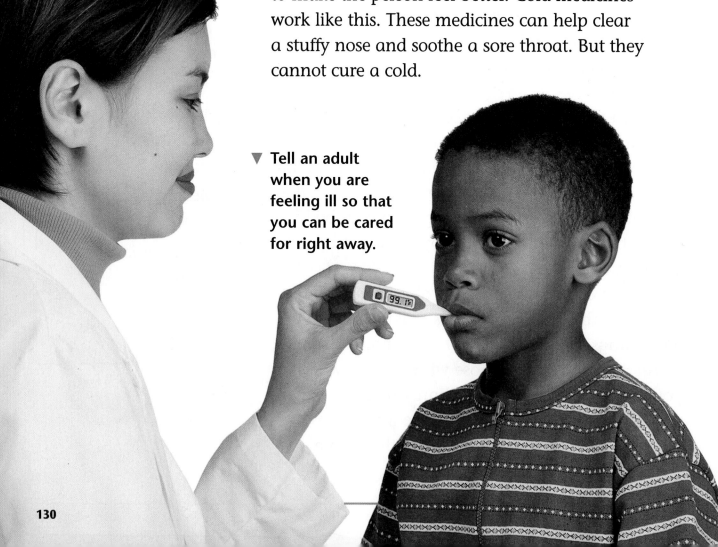

▼ **Tell an adult when you are feeling ill so that you can be cared for right away.**

130

Fever is a symptom of many diseases. To bring your temperature back to normal, an adult can give you a fever medicine. Some fever medicines are very safe for children to take. However, one kind—aspirin—is not safe for children. It can cause a serious illness in children. For this reason, take medicine only when a trusted adult gives it to you. The adult should read the labels or consult a doctor to decide which medicine to use, how much to give you, and how often you need it.

Take medicine only from a parent or other trusted adult.

▶ **This child is getting fever medicine. Fever medicines help the body temperature return to normal.**

LESSON CHECKUP

Check Your Facts

❶ What are two ways to prevent disease?

❷ What does it mean to be immune to a disease?

❸ CRITICAL THINKING If you feel ill, should you take medicine that another student gives to you? Why or why not?

Use Life Skills

❹ COMMUNICATE List three ways to keep from spreading or getting disease. Post your list where family members can see it.

Diseases You Can't Catch

You have been learning about infectious diseases. Infectious diseases are spread from one person to another by pathogens. Other diseases are not spread by pathogens. **Noninfectious diseases** cannot be caught from or spread to other persons. Some examples of noninfectious diseases are allergies, asthma, and diabetes.

What is an allergy?

One common noninfectious disease is an allergy. An **allergy** (A•ler•jee) is the body's reaction to some substance. People with allergies are not all allergic to the same things. Some people are allergic to just one thing. Other people are allergic to many things.

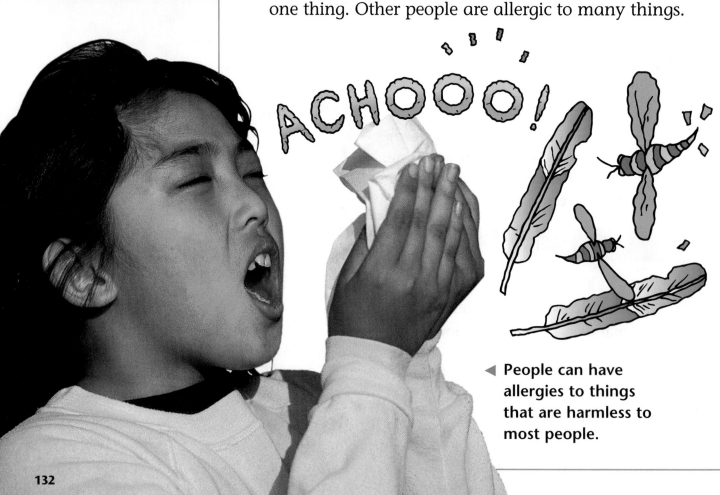

ACHOOO!

◀ People can have allergies to things that are harmless to most people.

Animals, plants, medicines, dust, bee stings, and foods can all cause allergies. Some foods that can cause allergies include eggs, peanuts, strawberries, wheat, and milk.

Not all people have allergies. Those who do have allergies have symptoms like sneezing, itchy and watery eyes, a runny nose, or an itchy skin rash. Some people have only mild symptoms. Others react strongly and may need to see a doctor right away. A very serious allergic reaction can cause death.

Doctors can help people with allergies. If you have an allergy to something, your doctor may tell you to stay away from it. Doctors can give medicine to help symptoms go away. They use skin tests to find out what things cause allergies. Sometimes people get allergy shots to reduce their symptoms.

Myth: Hay fever is a hay allergy.

Fact: Hay fever is an allergic reaction in the nose to pollen, animal skin, feathers, and molds carried in the air.

What is asthma?

Another noninfectious disease is asthma. **Asthma** (AZ•muh) causes people to have difficulty breathing. During an asthma attack, airways in the lungs become very narrow. This makes it hard for air to move in and out of the lungs. Compare the pictures below of the healthy airway and airway with asthma.

People who have asthma do not feel ill all the time. Their attacks are usually set off by allergies, exercise, or diseases that affect the lungs. Symptoms include tightness in the chest, difficulty breathing, and coughing and wheezing. Wheezing can be very loud and sometimes sounds squeaky.

Doctors can give medicine to help the symptoms of asthma go away. If you have asthma, your doctor may tell you to avoid the things that cause your asthma attacks.

The Respiratory System

Study the respiratory system found on pages 12 and 13 of The Amazing Human Body. Find the lungs in the picture. How does asthma affect these organs?

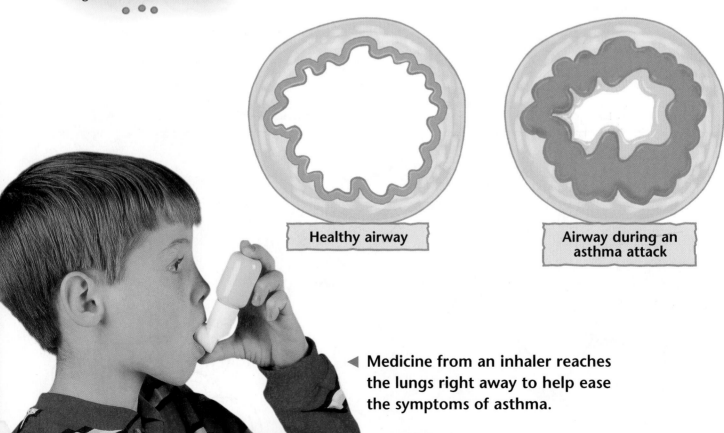

Healthy airway

Airway during an asthma attack

◀ Medicine from an inhaler reaches the lungs right away to help ease the symptoms of asthma.

What is diabetes?

Your digestive system changes some of the food you eat to a kind of sugar. The blood carries this sugar to the body cells. The cells use the sugar to make energy. **Diabetes** (dy•uh•BEE•teez) is a noninfectious disease that prevents the body from using sugar properly. The sugar doesn't go into the cells. Instead, it stays in the blood. Too much sugar in the blood can make people ill. They may feel very thirsty and tired and lose weight.

A doctor uses a blood test to find out if someone has diabetes. People with diabetes must eat a special diet. Often they must also take medicine. The medicine helps the body use the sugar from food.

Jill has just learned that she has diabetes. A home health nurse has come to help Jill and her mother. He shows them how to check the amount of sugar in Jill's blood. He talks to them about Jill's diet. He also shows Jill's mother how to give Jill medicine for her diabetes.

Career

Home Health Nurse

What They Do

Home health nurses go to patients' homes to observe their health, give medicines, give baths, and prepare meals. They may tell patients how to take medicine. They also may tell or show a patient's family how to take care of the patient.

Education and Training

Home health nurses must have some college education and training in nursing. Many states also require them to pass a special test. Home health nurses must have good communication skills, a desire to help others, and good judgment.

LESSON CHECKUP

Check Your Facts

1. What is an allergy?
2. What are some symptoms of asthma?
3. CRITICAL THINKING Why would someone with diabetes feel tired?

Use Life Skills

4. COMMUNICATE Choose one of the diseases described in the lesson. Imagine that you have this disease. Tell how it might affect your life.

Fighting Disease with a Healthful Lifestyle

You can do many things every day to keep your body healthy. Your lifestyle can make a difference in your health. *Lifestyle* refers to the choices a person makes about how to live his or her life. If you make healthful choices, then you have a healthful lifestyle. A healthful lifestyle helps your body fight disease.

How does the food you eat help you stay healthy?

Every morning for breakfast, Paul has orange juice and oatmeal with milk. Paul never feels tired during the school day. Lucas likes to have doughnuts and a soft drink for breakfast. Lucas is often sleepy at school.

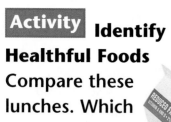 **Activity** **Identify Healthful Foods** Compare these lunches. Which lunch is more healthful? Make a list of other healthful lunches.

Which is healthful?

Always read labels.

◀ **Check the amounts of fat, sugar, and salt in foods. Eating less of these can help reduce your risk for some noninfectious diseases.**

The foods you choose to eat are important to your health. Food gives your body energy. Food also gives your body the things it needs to grow and fight disease.

Every day you should eat a variety of healthful foods. Use what you know about the Food Guide Pyramid to make smart choices about the foods you eat. When you make smart choices, your body gets the right amounts of nutrients and fiber.

If you choose foods that are not healthful, your body doesn't get the things it needs. You may have less energy, gain extra weight, and catch infectious diseases easily. If you eat a lot of foods low in fiber and high in fats, sugar, and salt, you may increase your risk of developing some noninfectious diseases, too.

At the grocery store you may have noticed foods labeled "fat-free," "sugar-free," or "low in salt." Are these foods really more healthful? The only way to know for sure is to read the labels on the food packages. Each food package is labeled with the amounts of fat, sugar, and salt in that food. By reading and comparing labels, you can find out which foods are more healthful.

CONSUMER
FOCUS

Analyze Advertising and Media Messages

Some packages might have bright colors, star characters, or certain words like "fat free" to try to get you to buy the product. Choose one of your favorite packaged foods. Look at the package, and list all the ways the package is being used to try to sell the food. Then read the label and decide if the food is healthful for your body. Use the steps on page *xv* to help you.

● ● ●

How does exercise help you stay healthy?

Jane's gym teacher always has the class begin with a jog around the playground. At first Jane couldn't make it all the way around. Now she can always finish. And she seems to have more energy.

Exercise is important to good health. It makes your muscles, heart, and lungs stronger. It helps your body use food and keeps you at a healthful weight. Exercise also helps your body fight disease.

JOURNAL

In your Health Journal, describe your favorite kinds of exercise. Tell when, where, and how often you do them. How do you feel after exercising? Remember that your journal is private.

Exercise helps you manage stress, too. You may be stressed when something makes you worried, nervous, angry, sad, or tired. You may also be stressed when things around you change or when you begin something new. Symptoms of stress include headache, stomachache, and trouble sleeping. Stress also can make your heart pound and your muscles feel tight. Too much stress can make you ill.

Exercise can help you feel calmer. It can help make the symptoms of stress go away. If you exercise regularly, your body will also handle stress better.

How does tobacco use affect a person's health?

Using tobacco is not a healthful lifestyle choice. When people smoke, they breathe tobacco smoke into their mouths, noses, throats, and lungs. Tobacco smoke has many harmful substances.

Smoking weakens the body. People who smoke are more likely to catch diseases such as colds and flu than those who don't smoke. People who use chewing tobacco usually have problems with their teeth and gums. Over time any kind of tobacco use may cause cancer, lung disease, and heart disease.

To have a healthful lifestyle, you must practice abstinence from tobacco. **Abstinence** (AB•stuh•nuhnts) means avoiding a behavior that will harm your health. Choosing not to use tobacco is one of the best things you can do for your health.

LIFE SKILLS
FOCUS

Refuse

Deborah's mom has asthma. A neighbor who is visiting asks Deborah's mom if she can smoke in the house. Use the steps for refusals shown on page *xi* to help Deborah's mom respond.

◄ When you breathe in other people's smoke, you get the same harmful substances that smokers breathe in. Many public places have made special areas for smokers. This helps keep the smoke away from nonsmokers.

LESSON CHECKUP

Check Your Facts

❶ List two healthful lifestyle choices.

❷ Why is it important to eat healthful foods?

❸ CRITICAL THINKING If you feel worried about a test that's coming up, what might make you feel better?

❹ CRITICAL THINKING Some of your friends think that smoking is cool. What should you tell them?

Set Health Goals

❺ Joe gets exercise one day a week. How can he change his lifestyle to make it more healthful?

MANAGE STRESS
to Control Disease

We all feel stress sometimes. Learning to manage stress will help keep you healthy.

Learn This Skill

Marcy has to give an oral report tomorrow, and she is feeling a lot of stress. She is sitting quietly, but her muscles feel tight, her heart is pounding, and her head hurts. Here are four things Marcy can do to manage her stress.

Exercise.

"Maybe I'll feel less tense if I go for a walk."

Imagine yourself doing well in the situation.

"I've had to give oral reports before. I'm usually nervous at first, but I always get through them."

Find a way to relax.

"Maybe I'll finish that book I was reading."

Talk to someone about how you're feeling.

"Maybe I'll call Maria. She always knows just what to say to make me feel better."

Practice This Skill

Here are some ways to help you solve the problems.

Ways to Manage Stress

- Exercise.
- Imagine yourself doing well in the situation.

- Find a way to relax.
- Talk to someone about how you're feeling.

A. Ann is worried about her first visit to the hospital to see her grandfather. She can feel her heart pounding. Use what you know about managing stress to help Ann.

B. Clay has a big math test tomorrow, and he can't get to sleep. Use what you know about managing stress to help Clay.

USE VOCABULARY

abstinence (p. 139)	diabetes (p. 135)	infectious disease (p. 124)	pathogens (p. 124)
allergy (p. 132)	disease (p. 122)	medicine (p. 130)	symptom (p. 122)
asthma (p. 134)	fever (p. 126)	noninfectious diseases	vaccine (p. 129)
bacteria (p. 124)	immune (p. 129)	(p. 132)	virus (p. 125)

Use the terms above to complete the sentences. Page numbers in ( ) tell you where to look in the chapter if you need help.

1. When a pathogen cannot make a person ill, that person is ____.

2. A body temperature that is higher than normal is called a ____.

3. The body's bad reaction to some substance is an ____.

4. One of the tiniest pathogens that cause diseases such as colds is a ____.

5. Something that causes the body not to work normally is a ____.

6. A liquid, powder, cream, spray, or pill used to treat illness is called ____.

7. ____ are simple living things made of just one cell.

8. A disease that prevents the body from using sugar properly is ____.

9. Germs that cause disease are called ____.

10. A sign such as a headache that something is wrong in the body is a ____.

11. Diseases, such as diabetes or asthma, that cannot be caught are ____.

12. A disease that causes people to have difficulty breathing sometimes is ____.

13. A substance given to keep you from getting a certain kind of disease is a ____.

14. A disease that can spread from one person to another is an ____.

15. You practice ____ when you avoid a behavior that will harm your health.

CHECK YOUR FACTS

Page numbers in ( ) tell you where to look in the chapter if you need help.

16. Tell what disease is. How do you know if you have a disease? (p. 122)

17. Name the two kinds of pathogens in the photos below, and tell how they cause infectious diseases. (p. 125)

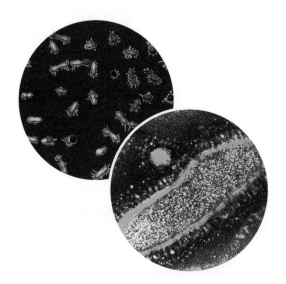

18. List three diseases that you can't catch. What are their symptoms? (pp. 132–135)

19. List two things that are part of a healthful lifestyle. Tell how they help you stay healthy. (pp. 136–138)

20. Name three ways you can prevent a disease from spreading. (pp. 128–129)

THINK CRITICALLY

21. Mike has the chicken pox. A virus causes chicken pox. Could Mike spread chicken pox to others? Explain.

22. Jenny eats many high-fat foods and rarely exercises. Explain how and why Jenny should change her lifestyle.

APPLY LIFE SKILLS

23. **Manage Stress** Suppose you will be playing soccer on a new team this year. How can you manage your stress to help you feel comfortable about playing on the new team?

24. **Communicate** Suppose your friend begins to feel ill at school. She wants to stay because there is a special program today. What would you tell her? How could you help her get care for her illness?

Promote Health **Home and Community**

1. Explain to your family what you have learned about how important exercise is for good health. Think of some ways family members can exercise together.
2. Make an advertisement that describes the importance of getting vaccines. Display the ad someplace in your school.

Activities

Health Collage

With a Partner • Look through old magazines to find pictures that show healthful lifestyle choices. Cut out these pictures. Use them to make a collage about healthful lifestyles. Be sure to give your collage a title.

Gathering Cheer

With a Team • Make a list of things other than medicine that would help an ill person feel better. If possible, gather these items together to make a "cheer-up kit." Send your kit to someone who is in the hospital or at home with an illness.

Disease Search

On Your Own • Find out more about smallpox. It is a dangerous infectious disease that many people died from until about 200 years ago. Write a paragraph about smallpox. Tell what causes it, what its symptoms are, and how it was stopped.

Germ Stoppers

At Home • Ask a family member to help you find items in the house that are used to kill pathogens. Find out how they are used to keep pathogens from spreading.

Multiple Choice

Choose the letter of the correct answer.

1. To treat a disease, your doctor might give you ____.
   a. diabetes   b. viruses
   c. medicine   d. pathogens

2. A fever is a ____, or a sign that something is wrong in the body.
   a. disease   b. pathogen
   c. lifestyle   d. symptom

3. Which health problem can be spread from one person to another?
   a. allergies   b. head lice
   c. asthma   d. diabetes

4. Choosing not to smoke is an example of ____.
   a. exercise   b. abstinence
   c. diet   d. studying

5. A disease that causes people to have difficulty breathing is ____.
   a. strep throat   b. diabetes
   c. asthma   d. cancer

Modified True or False

Write *true* or *false*. If a sentence is false, replace the underlined term to make the sentence true.

6. You are immune to a disease when its pathogen <u>cannot</u> make you ill.

7. <u>Food</u> gives your body things it needs to grow and fight disease.

8. <u>Asthma</u> is a disease that prevents the body from using sugar properly.

9. A <u>disease</u> is something that causes the body not to work normally.

10. Using tobacco is a <u>healthful</u> lifestyle choice.

11. A <u>pathogen</u> is given to keep you from getting a certain kind of disease.

12. An <u>allergy</u> is the body's reaction to some substance.

13. An infectious disease <u>can</u> be spread from one person to another.

Short Answer

Write a complete sentence to answer each question.

14. Name two ways to prevent disease.

15. What are some ways that infectious diseases are spread?

16. What does exercise do for the body?

17. Describe how smoking affects the body.

18. Why should you tell an adult when you are feeling ill?

Writing in Health

Write paragraphs to answer each item.

19. Samantha is going to perform in her first play. Describe how she can manage her stress and relax.

20. Explain why living a healthful lifestyle helps prevent disease.

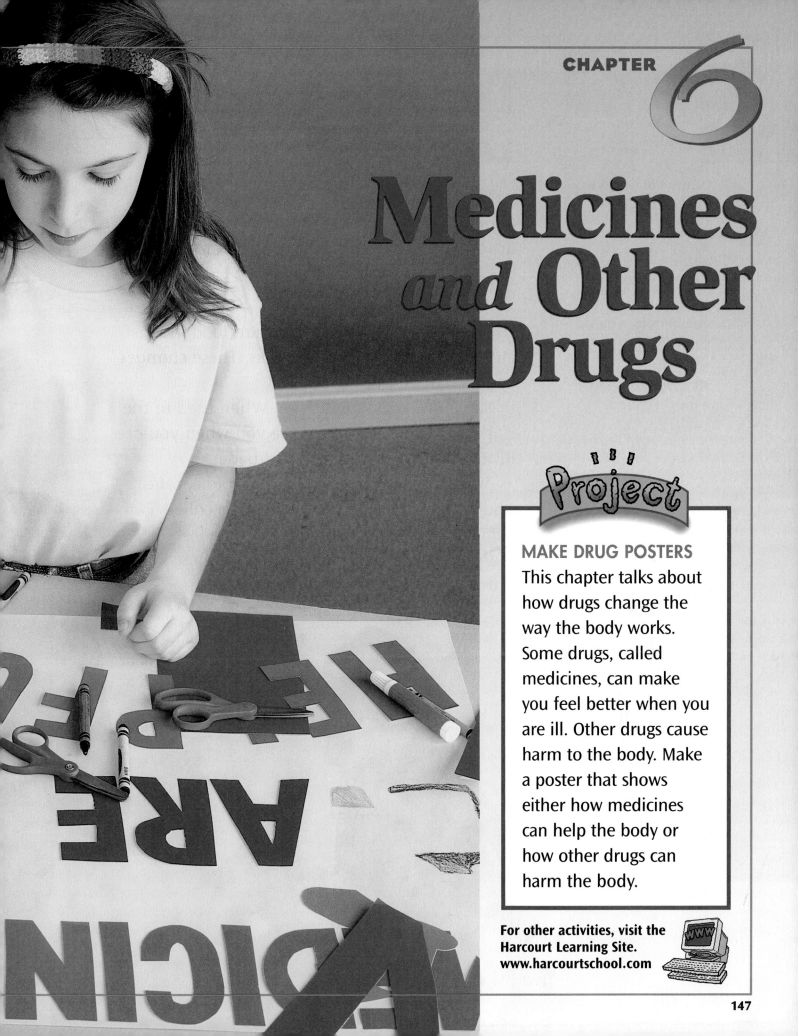

Medicines and Other Drugs

Project

MAKE DRUG POSTERS

This chapter talks about how drugs change the way the body works. Some drugs, called medicines, can make you feel better when you are ill. Other drugs cause harm to the body. Make a poster that shows either how medicines can help the body or how other drugs can harm the body.

For other activities, visit the Harcourt Learning Site.
www.harcourtschool.com

MAIN IDEA
Drugs change the way the body works. They can help you or harm you.

WHY LEARN THIS? Knowing the difference between helpful and harmful drugs will help keep you healthy.

VOCABULARY
• drug

Learning About Drugs

Some drugs can help you when you are ill. Other drugs can make you ill. Do you know which drugs are helpful and which are harmful?

What are drugs?

A **drug** is something other than food that changes the way the body works. These changes can be helpful or harmful.

Some drugs are medicines. When used in the right way, medicines can cure you when you are ill. They can also help you feel better.

Some foods and drinks, like chocolate, coffee, and some soft drinks contain a drug called caffeine. Caffeine makes some people feel more awake. But caffeine can also be harmful if you have too much.

▼ Medicines can help you when you are ill or in pain. This spray is a medicine that kills bacteria on the skin.

SOCIAL STUDIES
CONNECTION

Ancient Medicines

On Your Own Long ago Native Americans found that drinking tea made from the bark of a willow tree took away pain. The bark contains the same chemical that is in aspirin. Find out about other ancient medicines.

• • •

◄ Many products around the home contain dangerous substances. The warning labels on these containers warn the products should only be used as directed.

Some drugs, like marijuana and cocaine, are harmful. They change the way people think, feel, and act. They can also make people very ill. Because they are so harmful, marijuana and cocaine are illegal. It is against the law for anyone to buy, sell, have, or use them.

Many household products give off dangerous fumes. Some people use the fumes as a drug. They sniff the fumes to get high. A "high" is a common way of describing how people feel when they use drugs. But the fumes are poisons that can cause illness, brain damage, or even death.

LESSON CHECKUP

Check Your Facts

❶ What do drugs do to the body?

❷ CRITICAL THINKING All medicines are drugs. But are all drugs medicines? Explain your answer.

❸ How can household products be dangerous?

Set Health Goals

❹ Make a list of items in your home that might contain warnings on the label. Why do you think it is important for warnings to be listed on the items?

MAIN IDEA
Medicines can help you get well when you use them correctly.

WHY LEARN THIS? You can find out how different medicines can help you.

VOCABULARY
- over-the-counter medicine
- prescription medicine

Medicines and Their Uses

When you get ill, an adult may give you medicine to help you get better. How do grown-ups know what kind of medicine you need? Where does it come from?

What are the different kinds of medicine?

There are two kinds of medicines. An **over-the-counter medicine** (OTC medicine) is a medicine that an adult can buy without a doctor's order. Drugstores and grocery stores sell OTC medicines. OTC medicines are for minor health problems, such as sore throats, colds, and headaches. Cough syrups, pain relievers, and first-aid sprays are all OTC medicines. The label on an

▼ There are thousands of over-the-counter medicines. An adult can buy these medicines without a doctor's order.

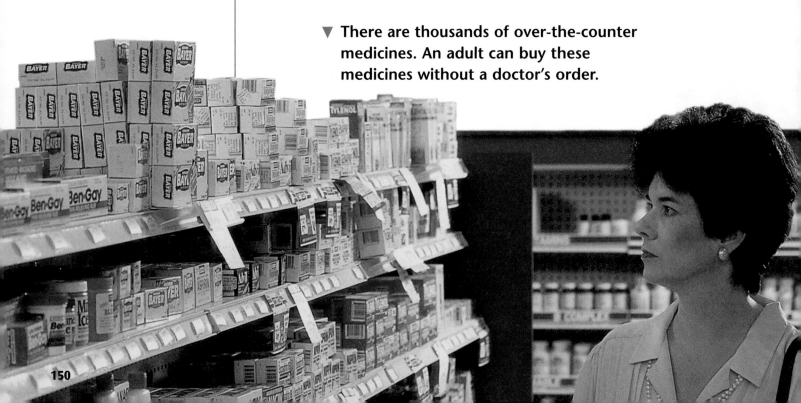

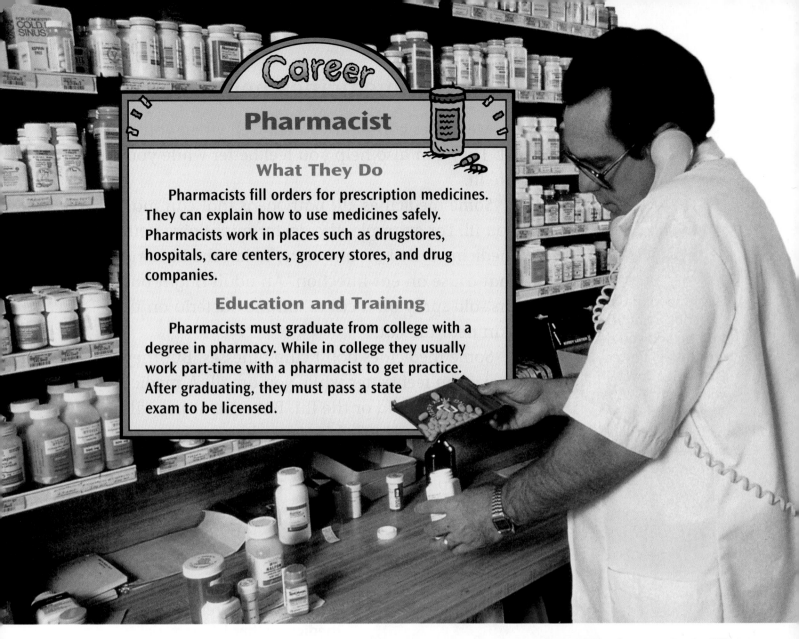

Career

Pharmacist

What They Do

Pharmacists fill orders for prescription medicines. They can explain how to use medicines safely. Pharmacists work in places such as drugstores, hospitals, care centers, grocery stores, and drug companies.

Education and Training

Pharmacists must graduate from college with a degree in pharmacy. While in college they usually work part-time with a pharmacist to get practice. After graduating, they must pass a state exam to be licensed.

▲ **This pharmacist is filling a prescription.**

OTC medicine tells what the medicine treats. It also gives directions for using the medicine. Adults must always follow these directions exactly so the medicine will be used safely.

A **prescription medicine** (prih•SKRIP•shuhn MEH•duh•suhn) is a medicine that must be ordered by a doctor. A doctor writes the order, called a prescription. Then a pharmacist fills the order.

Prescription medicines are strong and must be used correctly. That is why a doctor must order them. A doctor or pharmacist can explain exactly how to use them.

How can medicines help you?

Medicines can help you get well when you are ill. They can also help you feel better while you are ill.

Some medicines kill pathogens that can make you ill. For example, the doctor might give you a medicine called an antibiotic to kill the bacteria that cause an ear infection. An adult might put a first-aid spray on a cut to kill the bacteria on the skin near the cut.

Some medicines don't cure illnesses. But they make you feel better while you are ill. A medicine won't cure a cold or the flu. But a medicine will make a headache feel better or lower a fever caused by the flu. One medicine children your age should *not* take is aspirin. Aspirin is only safe for adults. Aspirin can cause an illness in children that can lead to death.

▼ Antibiotics are prescription medicines that kill bacterial pathogens. This mother is giving her child an antibiotic to help cure an ear infection.

◀ Some OTC medicines can help when you are in pain. There are many different kinds of pain relievers.

Medicines come in many different forms. There are pills, liquids, sprays, and creams. Some pills can be chewed. Other pills are swallowed whole. Some liquid medicines are meant to be swallowed. Other liquids, creams, and sprays are put directly on the area being treated. All medicines should always be given by an adult.

LESSON CHECKUP

Check Your Facts

1 Name the two kinds of medicines.

2 Which kind of medicine can an adult buy without a doctor's prescription?

3 CRITICAL THINKING Why must a pharmacist be able to read a doctor's prescription?

4 CRITICAL THINKING Can a medicine help you even if it does not cure you? Give an example.

Use Life Skills

5 MAKE DECISIONS Often OTC medicines help a person feel better. Sometimes a prescribed medicine is more helpful. Make a list of reasons why a doctor might decide to write an order for a prescription.

MAIN IDEA
Medicine can harm the body if it is used in the wrong way.

WHY LEARN THIS? Using medicine correctly will help you stay healthy.

VOCABULARY
• side effects

How Can Medicines Be Used Safely?

Medicines can help you when you are ill. But they can also be harmful if used in the wrong way. Always remember to follow the rules when you must use a medicine.

OPEN

PUSH DOWN & TURN

CLOSE

Safety Rules for Medicine Use

Be careful! Medicines can be dangerous.

- Only an adult should give you medicine. Never take a medicine on your own.
- Always follow the directions on the medicine label.
- Never take someone else's prescription medicine.
- Don't use old medicines. They can change when they get old and make you ill. Look at the date on the label.
- Leave the labels on all medicines.
- Keep medicines on high shelves in locked cabinets.
- Keep medicines away from small children.

LIFE SKILLS
FOCUS

Refuse

Bryan started sneezing while he was playing at Linda's home. Linda offered Bryan some of her prescription allergy medicine. Tell ways that Bryan could refuse this offer. Use the steps for refusing shown on page *xi*.

● ● ●

◀ Medicines on store shelves have safety seals. The seals keep the medicines clean. They also stop other people from opening the medicine before someone buys it. Never buy medicine with a broken safety seal.

What should you do when you think you need a medicine? Tell a trusted adult! An adult can help you. Before buying a medicine, an adult should check the safety seal. The seal should not be broken. An adult should give you the correct amount listed on the label, not more and not less. Watch for any side effects. **Side effects** are unwanted changes in the body caused by a medicine. If you feel any side effects, such as dizziness, itching, or a headache, tell a trusted adult.

Activity **Follow Medicine Safety Rules**
Read the safety rules on page 154. Then look at the pictures on pages 152 and 153. How are the people in the pictures following the safety rules? What are some other safety rules you should follow?

LESSON CHECKUP

Check Your Facts

1. What does the label on a medicine do?
2. Why should you never use old medicines?
3. CRITICAL THINKING Why should you be careful when taking medicines?
4. What are side effects?

Set Health Goals

5. Make a small poster listing the safety rules for medicine. Put it up at home where medicines are kept. How can the poster help you use medicines safely?

What Is Caffeine?

Do you enjoy iced tea, chocolate, and soft drinks? Many people do. But watch out! Some of these items contain caffeine. **Caffeine** (ka•FEEN) is a drug that speeds up the heart. Some OTC medicines contain caffeine, too.

It is not harmful to take in a small amount of caffeine. Many adults drink coffee in the morning. It helps them feel more awake. But large amounts of caffeine can make adults feel jittery. Smaller amounts of caffeine can keep children from sleeping. Too much caffeine also can strain the heart and upset the stomach.

It is hard for people who take in a lot of caffeine to stop using it. When they don't have caffeine, they can get tired and upset. They might also get headaches.

▼ Caffeine is in many drinks and foods, such as coffee, tea, and chocolate. Colas and fruit-flavored soft drinks often contain caffeine, too.

◀ Does your favorite drink have caffeine? Look for drinks that are labeled "caffeine-free."

CONSUMER FOCUS

Access Valid Health Information
Use the Internet or other sources to find out how much caffeine is in soft drinks. Make a list of at least five different soft drinks. Next to each one, write how many milligrams of caffeine the soft drink contains. Use the steps on page *xvi* to help you decide whether the sources are reliable.

• • •

How can you avoid caffeine?

Many people drink a lot of soft drinks filled with caffeine or eat a lot of chocolate. They may not even know that they are taking in caffeine. If you know which foods have caffeine, you can avoid letting caffeine become a habit.

Chocolate, coffee, tea, and soft drinks often have caffeine. If you often eat or drink foods with caffeine, try to find foods without caffeine instead.

LESSON CHECKUP

Check Your Facts
❶ List four sources of caffeine.
❷ Why should people limit caffeine?
❸ CRITICAL THINKING Name four drinks that don't have caffeine.

Set Health Goals
❹ Cola drinks and many other soft drinks contain caffeine. Think about the drinks you've had in the last two days. List the ones that contain caffeine. If you drank several drinks with caffeine, think about what you can do to cut back on the amount of caffeine you take in each day.

Inhalants and Other Drugs

You probably know about harmful drugs such as marijuana and cocaine. But did you know that some household products are also dangerous drugs?

What are inhalants?

You walk into the bathroom and know right away that it has been cleaned recently. How do you know? You smell the fumes from the cleaning products. You can also smell fumes at a gas station.

Some people breathe in fumes from products such as spray paints, glues, markers, cleaners, and nail polish remover. These people are trying to get high. This can be very dangerous. The fumes are poisons. Substances that give off fumes are **inhalants** (in•HAY•luhnts). Labels on inhalants warn people to avoid breathing them.

▶ You must use some glues only where there is a lot of fresh air. Look at the label for warnings when you use glue.

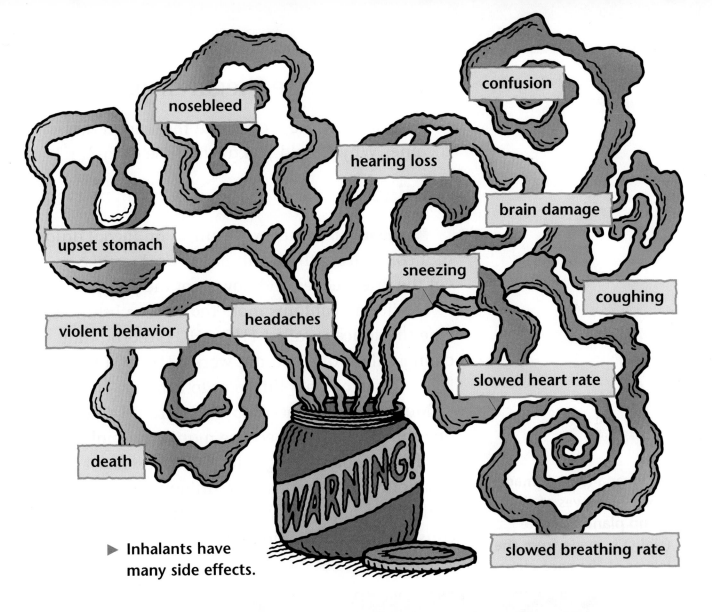

confusion

nosebleed

hearing loss

brain damage

upset stomach

sneezing

coughing

violent behavior

headaches

slowed heart rate

death

slowed breathing rate

▶ Inhalants have many side effects.

Inhalants distort how you see, hear, and feel. Yet many people do not think of inhalants as drugs because many inhalants are sold as common household products.

Inhaling the fumes can cause nosebleeds and headaches. Inhalants can cause brain damage. Inhalants can also slow your heart and breathing rates, which can kill you. Many people have died instantly by breathing in too much of the poisonous fumes at one time.

HUMAN BODY

C O N N E C T I O N

Inhalants

Study the picture showing how inhalants affect the body. List all the organs of the body that inhalants affect. Find these organs in the human body diagrams on pages 1–15 at the front of the book.

● ● ●

What are some illegal drugs?

Do you know the facts about marijuana and cocaine? Why should you avoid these drugs?

Marijuana

Marijuana (mair•uh•WAH•nuh) is an illegal drug that comes from the hemp plant. Users smoke or eat the dried leaves and flowers of the plant.

Marijuana contains more than 400 substances. One substance is called THC. THC is a drug that changes the way the brain works. THC can make it hard to remember things or to learn.

Marijuana can speed up the heart. It can cause breathing problems. Because marijuana makes it hard for the body to fight infections, users get ill more often than nonusers. Marijuana can also make users nervous. When it is smoked, it can cause cancer, just as cigarettes do.

▼ Marijuana (left) is made from the leaves of the hemp plant. Cocaine (right) is made from the leaves of the coca plant.

▲ It is against the law to have, use, sell, or buy cocaine or marijuana. People who use these drugs can go to jail.

Cocaine

Cocaine (koh•KAYN) is an illegal drug made from the leaves of the coca plant. Most users sniff powdered cocaine. Some users inject it with a needle. Others smoke a strong form of cocaine, called "crack."

Cocaine can make people feel good for five to forty minutes. Then users often feel sad, nervous, confused, angry, or tired. They want to use more and more of the drug to get the same feeling back.

Cocaine users may get dizzy. Cocaine can also cause lung or brain damage. Even one use of cocaine can cause a stroke, heart attack, or death.

LESSON CHECKUP

Check Your Facts

1. CRITICAL THINKING Why is it a good idea to turn on a fan when using certain types of glue?

2. List two products that people misuse as inhalants.

3. What are the harmful effects of marijuana?

4. What are the harmful effects of cocaine?

Use Life Skills

5. REFUSE Make a list of the harmful effects of inhalants. Keep this list in mind if anyone asks you to try an inhalant.

How Can I Say *No* to Drugs?

Sometime someone may ask you to try a drug. It is important to decide ahead of time how to refuse. To **refuse** is to say *no*.

You can practice ways to refuse with your family or friends. You might say something like, "I want to have fun, not hurt my body" or "I can have fun without it." Think of something that feels right for you. Then you will be ready if someone asks you to use drugs.

▶ Avoid dangerous drugs. Get involved in an activity you enjoy instead, like sports, music, or art.

▲ More and more kids are saying *no* to drugs.

LIFE SKILLS
FOCUS

Communicate

Cathy's friend told her that someone on the playground had drugs. Cathy's friend said she might like to try the drugs. What should Cathy say to her friend? Use the steps for communicating shown on page *xii*.

• • •

If you have doubts about saying *no*, remember how harmful drugs can be. A person can go to jail for using drugs. Drugs can change the way the brain works so a person cannot think well. They can cause illness and even death.

Some people use drugs to get high or to escape from their problems. But the high feeling doesn't last long. When that feeling wears off, users feel very low. And their problems are still there.

If someone asks you to use drugs, say *no*. Then talk to a trusted adult about it. That adult can be a family member, teacher, or doctor. You do not have to face the problem alone.

LESSON CHECKUP

Check Your Facts

❶ CRITICAL THINKING Why should you choose friends who don't use drugs?

❷ What should you remember if you have doubts about saying *no* to drugs?

❸ Whom can you talk to for help if someone asks you to try drugs?

Use Life Skills

❹ REFUSE Make a list of three ways you can say *no* to drugs.

REFUSE
Inhalants

There may be a time when someone asks you to use drugs. Know ahead of time how to refuse.

Learn This Skill

Kamil went shopping with his friend Roger. They were looking at art supplies. Roger opened a tube of glue and started sniffing it. He wanted Kamil to try it.

1. Say *no*.

"Try it. It will make you feel really weird," Roger says.
"No," says Kamil.

2. State your reasons for saying *no*.

Warning—Sniffing glue can cause brain damage.

"I don't want to fry my brain!" says Kamil.

3. Suggest something else to do.

"I want to look for some new paintbrushes," Kamil says.

4. Repeat *no*; walk away.

"I don't want to be anywhere near that stuff!" Kamil says as he walks away.

Practice This Skill

Use the steps to help you solve the problems below.

> **Steps for Refusing**
>
> **1.** Say *no*.
> **2.** State your reasons for saying *no*.
> **3.** Suggest something else to do.
> **4.** Repeat *no*; walk away.

A. Marta is visiting her cousin Jane. Jane has found some pills in her mother's purse. She wants Marta to try them with her. How can Jane refuse?

B. Tara's older brother Mike wants her to try some pills that will give her more energy. How can Tara say *no*?

USE VOCABULARY

caffeine (p. 156)   inhalants (p. 158)   prescription medicine (p. 151)

cocaine (p. 161)   marijuana (p. 160)   refuse (p. 162)

drug (p. 148)   over-the-counter medicine (p. 150)   side effects (p. 155)

Use the terms above to complete the sentences. Page numbers in ( ) tell you where to look in the chapter if you need help.

1. The unwanted changes in the body caused by a medicine are ____.

2. An illegal drug made from the leaves of the coca plant is ____.

3. Something other than food that changes the way your body works is a ____.

4. Coffee and chocolate contain ____, a drug that speeds up the heart.

5. A medicine that an adult can get only with a doctor's order is a ____.

6. To say *no* is to ____.

7. An illegal drug that comes from the hemp plant is ____.

8. ____ are substances that give off dangerous fumes and are sometimes used as drugs.

9. A medicine that an adult can buy without a prescription is an ____.

CHECK YOUR FACTS

Page numbers in ( ) tell you where to look in the chapter if you need help.

10. What are medicines? (p. 148)

11. What does the label on an OTC medicine tell you? (pp. 150–151)

12. What is a prescription medicine? (p. 151)

13. List two possible side effects of medicine. (p. 155)

14. List two foods that contain caffeine. (p. 156)

15. List four side effects people may develop if they misuse the products shown here. (p. 159)

16. Which substance in marijuana changes the way the brain works? (p. 160)

17. Name a fun activity that does not include the use of drugs. (p. 162)

18. Why is it important to read the labels on over-the-counter medicines?

19. Illegal drugs, such as marijuana and cocaine, are dangerous. Why do some people use them anyway?

20. Why should you read warning labels on substances such as glue?

APPLY LIFE SKILLS

21. **Refuse** You go to a party at a friend's house. After a while many of the people go into the basement to sniff glue. They tell you to try it. Everyone is looking at you, waiting for your answer. How would you refuse?

22. **Communicate** You can refuse drugs when someone offers them to you. But how can you communicate to others that they should never offer drugs to you?

Promote Health **Home and Community**

1. Look at the place where your family stores medicines. Is it safe, according to the Safety Rules for Medicine Use? If so, why? If not, where can your family store the medicine more safely?

2. Make a poster that tells other kids to stay off drugs. Hang your poster up in the classroom.

Activities

Safety Cartoons

At Home • Look at the Safety Rules for Medicine Use shown here. Pick one. Then draw a cartoon to illustrate the rule. Print the rule at the bottom of the drawing. Display your cartoon with those of your classmates.

Drug Messages

With a Partner • How do ads and TV programs show the use of alcohol and other drugs? Watch several TV programs and ads. Take notes. What messages do these shows and ads send to kids about alcohol and other drugs? Report to your class.

Safety Rules for Medicine Use

- Only an adult should give you medicine. Never take a medicine on your own.
- Always follow the directions on the medicine label.
- Never take someone else's prescription medicine.
- Don't use old medicines. They can change when they get old and make you ill. Look at the date on the label.
- Leave the labels on all medicines.
- Keep medicines on high shelves in locked cabinets.
- Keep medicines away from small children.

Antidrug Party

With a Group • Plan a party or rally at your school to celebrate saying *no* to drugs. Think of fun activities for the celebration. Include music and food. Ask speakers to take part. Make posters and buttons with antidrug messages. Show that you can have lots of fun without drugs—and that most kids don't want to use them.

Talk to Your Pharmacist

On Your Own • Talk with a pharmacist about his or her job. What do pharmacists do each day? Is the work fun? How did he or she become a pharmacist? Write down what the pharmacist says, or record the interview. Share what you find out with your class.

Multiple Choice

Choose the letter of the correct answer.

1. Drugs change the way the body ____.
   a. looks   b. works
   c. tastes   d. smells

2. Pharmacists prepare ____ medicines.
   a. no   b. OTC
   c. prescription   d. all

3. Caffeine is a drug that ____ the heart.
   a. speeds up   b. destroys
   c. slows down   d. copies

4. The fumes that come from inhalants are ____.
   a. poisons   b. medicines
   c. safe   d. air

5. It is important to decide ahead of time how to ____ drugs.
   a. accept   b. buy
   c. try   d. refuse

Modified True or False

Write *true* or *false*. If a sentence is false, replace the underlined term to make the sentence true.

6. Drugs can change the way people <u>think</u>, feel, and act.

7. A <u>doctor</u> uses a prescription to fill a medicine order.

8. Some over-the-counter medicines <u>relieve pain</u> or stop coughs.

9. Never take someone else's <u>medicine</u>.

10. Always read the <u>safety seal</u> on a medicine.

11. Caffeine is in coffee and some <u>soft drinks</u>.

12. Marijuana is an illegal drug that comes from the <u>corn</u> plant.

13. Cocaine use can cause <u>brain</u> damage.

Short Answer

Write a complete sentence to answer each question.

14. What kinds of health problems do over-the-counter medicines treat?

15. Why should you always leave the labels on medicines?

16. How can you cut down the amount of caffeine in your diet?

17. List some of the harmful effects that marijuana can have on the body.

18. How can inhalants harm the body?

Writing in Health

Write paragraphs to answer each item.

19. What is the safe way to take medicine?

20. What could happen to someone who uses drugs?

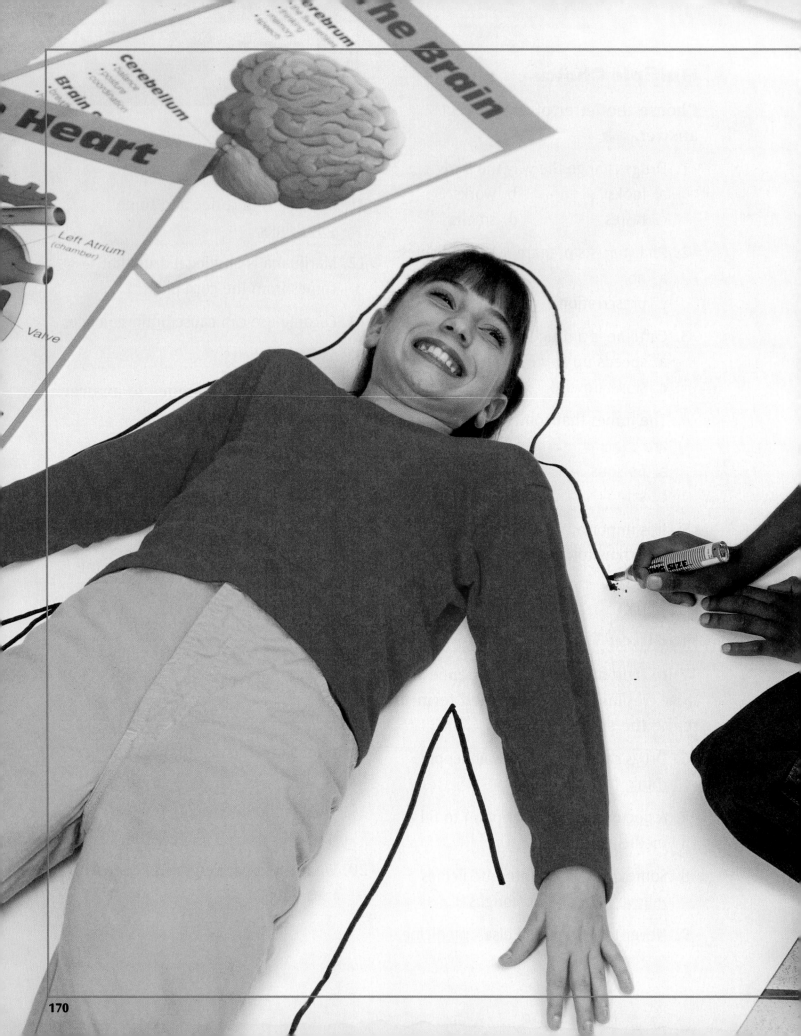

Avoiding Alcohol and Tobacco

MAKE A MODEL With a small group, make a life-size model of the human body on cardboard or drawing paper. On the model, draw the body organs that are affected by alcohol and tobacco.

For other activities, visit the Harcourt Learning Site. www.harcourtschool.com

MAIN IDEA
Alcohol and tobacco are harmful drugs.

WHY LEARN THIS? Knowing the dangers of alcohol and tobacco will help you avoid using them.

VOCABULARY
• nicotine
• alcohol

Learning About Tobacco and Alcohol

You may have seen adults using tobacco (tuh•BA•koh) or alcohol (AL•kuh•hawl) products. You may think these products are safe to use. But did you know that tobacco and alcohol are drugs? Drugs change the way a person's body works. Tobacco and alcohol can harm a person who uses them.

Why are tobacco and alcohol drugs?

The tobacco in cigarettes and cigars comes from the leaves of the tobacco plant. Tobacco that is smoked in pipes is made from the same leaves. Other tobacco products are chewed or sucked. These products look different, but they all contain tobacco.

Types of Tobacco

snuff

smoking tobacco

chewing tobacco

► Smoking tobacco includes cigarettes, cigars, and loose tobacco smoked in pipes. Snuff and chewing tobacco are smokeless tobacco products.

172

All tobacco products have nicotine. **Nicotine** (NIH•kuh•teen) is a drug in tobacco. People who use tobacco products are putting this drug into their bodies. Like other drugs, nicotine causes changes in the body. Some drugs, such as the medicines a doctor gives, cause good changes. The changes nicotine causes are not good.

Nicotine is a poison. Farmers and gardeners use it to kill insects on plants. Nicotine can kill people, too. A small amount of pure nicotine—about a tablespoonful—can kill an adult. Smaller amounts harm the body. Many tobacco users know that tobacco can make them ill. But the nicotine also makes them keep wanting tobacco.

Alcohol is also a drug. Like nicotine, alcohol causes changes in the user's body. Alcohol is found in drinks such as beer, wine, and mixed drinks. Some adult liquid medicines also have alcohol. Most children's medicines are made so that they have no alcohol.

Drinking alcohol is harmful, especially for children. Using alcohol for many years also causes health problems. Some people who use alcohol can't stop using it without help. They can get the help they need at programs in local clinics, hospitals, and treatment centers. Alcoholics Anonymous, Rational Recovery, and Al-Anon are also places they and their families can go for help.

Types of Alcohol

beer

wine

mixed drinks

LESSON CHECKUP

Check Your Facts

① What drug is found in beer, wine, and mixed drinks?

② CRITICAL THINKING Most people know that tobacco and alcohol can harm the body. Why do people still use these drugs?

③ Name a drug found in tobacco.

Set Health Goals

④ List three reasons to avoid using tobacco and alcohol. Then write ways you can keep from using these drugs.

MAIN IDEA Many things in tobacco harm the user.

WHY LEARN THIS? Knowing how dangerous tobacco is will help you refuse to use it.

VOCABULARY
• addiction
• chewing tobacco
• smokeless tobacco
• tar
• cancer
• environmental tobacco smoke

How Tobacco Affects the Body

All kinds of tobacco have nicotine in them. Nicotine can get into the body through smoke or through juice from the tobacco.

Nicotine can cause addiction. **Addiction** (uh•DIK•shuhn) is a constant need that makes people keep using drugs even when they want to stop. Nicotine affects the way the brain works. It also makes the heart beat faster and harder and can cause heart disease.

How do people use tobacco?

Most people who use tobacco smoke it. Some smoke it in a pipe or cigar. Most smoke it in cigarettes. To make smoking tobacco, the green leaves of the tobacco plant are dried. Then the dried tobacco leaves are shredded. Pipe tobacco and the tobacco in cigars look similar to the tobacco in cigarettes. The outside of a cigar is made from tobacco leaves that have not been shredded.

Some people chew small wads—or plugs—of moist tobacco. This moist tobacco for chewing is called **chewing tobacco**.

Some people put clumps of powdered or shredded tobacco between their cheeks and gums and suck it. This tobacco is called **smokeless tobacco**, or snuff.

◄ Some people think chewing tobacco is safer than smoking it. It's not! Nicotine in the tobacco still gets into the body.

How does tobacco affect the body?

Tobacco smoke has more than 4,000 different things in it. Many of these things can harm a person's body. You have already learned how harmful nicotine is. Tobacco smoke also contains tar. **Tar** is a dark, sticky substance. It coats the lungs and air passages of people who breathe in tobacco smoke. Tar makes breathing hard. It can also lead to lung diseases and **cancer** (KAN•ser), a disease that makes cells grow wildly. Other problems that tobacco causes are shown in the diagram below.

Your Lungs

Your lungs are part of your respiratory system. To learn more about how your lungs get air in and out of your body, turn to pages 12 and 13. How would tobacco smoke travel through your body?

Mouth Using tobacco causes bad breath. Smokeless tobacco stains the users' teeth. It makes their gums and lips crack and bleed. It can lead to mouth cancer.

Throat Smoking causes coughing. It can cause throat cancer.

Heart Nicotine makes blood vessels shrink. The heart beats faster and harder. This can lead to heart disease.

Lungs Tar coats smokers' lungs. They have trouble getting enough air. Smokers may die from lung cancer or other lung diseases.

▲ This girl isn't smoking. But smoke from the pipe and cigar in the room is affecting her. The ETS harms her eyes, nose, throat, and lungs.

How is tobacco harmful to people who don't use it?

Have you ever been in a room with someone who was smoking? If so, you could probably see smoke in the air.

The smoke that fills a room when someone is smoking is called **environmental tobacco smoke** (in•vy•ruhn•MEN•tuhl tuh•BA•koh SMOHK), or *ETS*. Some ETS comes directly from burning cigarettes, pipes, or cigars. The rest is smoke that is breathed out by smokers.

ETS carries poisons that can hurt people who breathe it—even if they don't smoke themselves. Some people live or work in places filled with ETS. These people may become ill more often than people who live and work in smoke-free places.

Adults and children who live in homes with ETS may get more colds, coughs, and sore throats than those who do not live with smokers. Nonsmokers who breathe ETS for many years may get the same diseases as smokers. They have a higher risk of getting lung diseases, heart diseases, and cancer than people who live or work in smoke-free places.

One way you can avoid ETS is to sit in the nonsmoking section of a restaurant. You can have an adult politely ask people sitting near you not to smoke. If necessary, leave a room where many people are smoking.

JOURNAL

Have you ever been in a room where ETS bothered you? In your Health Journal, write about ways other people's smoke has affected you. Tell what you might have done to solve the problem.

Cough! Cough! Please don't smoke!

Activity **Avoid ETS** Imagine you are in a place where people are smoking. Suggest ways you could protect your health from ETS. Tell what you might do or say. Be sure your suggestions are polite!

LESSON CHECKUP

Check Your Facts

1. List four products that have tobacco in them.
2. Name two substances in tobacco smoke that can harm you.
3. CRITICAL THINKING How can you be harmed by tobacco even if you don't smoke?
4. How does nicotine affect the heart of a tobacco user?

Set Health Goals

5. List three things you like to do that require a strong heart and lungs. How would smoking affect your ability to do these activities?

MAIN IDEA Any amount of alcohol is dangerous for young people.

WHY LEARN THIS? Knowing how dangerous alcohol is will help you refuse it.

VOCABULARY
• bloodstream
• alcoholism

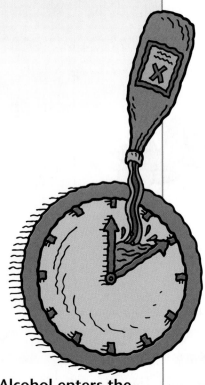

▲ Alcohol enters the bloodstream from the stomach and small intestine. Within a few minutes it reaches the brain and other parts of the body.

How Alcohol Affects the Body

Drinking alcohol regularly can be harmful. An adult who drinks too much alcohol can have serious health problems. Alcohol is especially harmful to young people, because they are still growing.

What happens when a person drinks alcohol?

Most food you eat has to be digested. It takes several hours for food to travel through your digestive system. Chemicals there break food into nutrients. Nutrients move from your digestive system to your bloodstream. Your **bloodstream** is the blood flowing through your body. Look on pages 10–11 to see how your bloodstream carries nutrients to all parts of your body.

Alcohol doesn't need to be digested. It begins to enter the bloodstream as soon as it reaches the stomach and small intestine. Just minutes after a person drinks alcohol, the alcohol has traveled to all parts of the body.

Alcohol slows down the brain's ability to collect information. It also slows down the messages the brain sends to other parts of the body. After drinking alcohol, the user might find it hard to walk or speak. He or she cannot see clearly. Making decisions isn't easy. Paying attention or remembering things becomes hard, too.

Alcohol can even change the user's personality. Different people change in different ways. Some people get silly when they drink alcohol. Others feel sad. Still others become loud or angry.

Often people who drink too much feel sleepy. People who drink too much may also get dizzy. Sometimes the dizziness is so bad it makes them ill. They may still feel ill the next day. Many people get headaches after they drink. These headaches can last a few hours or a whole day.

Alcohol in the Body

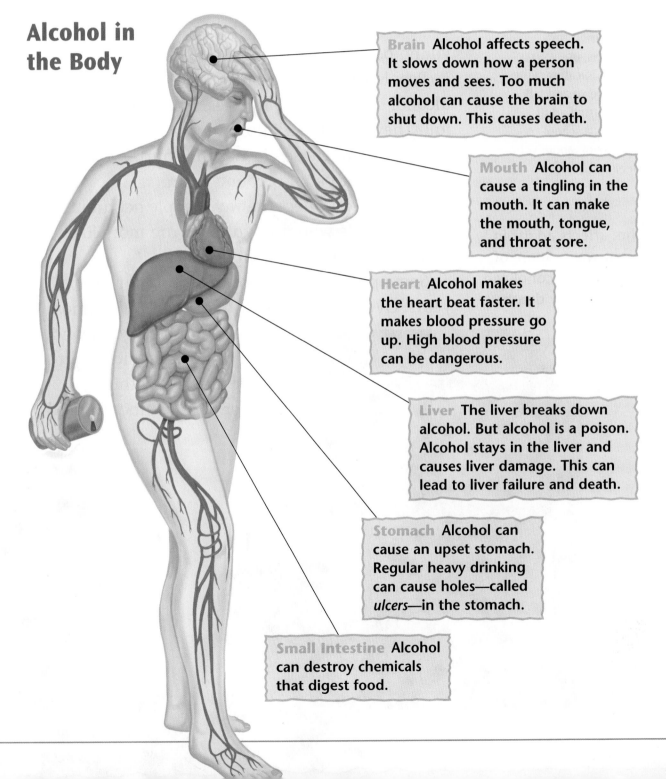

Brain Alcohol affects speech. It slows down how a person moves and sees. Too much alcohol can cause the brain to shut down. This causes death.

Mouth Alcohol can cause a tingling in the mouth. It can make the mouth, tongue, and throat sore.

Heart Alcohol makes the heart beat faster. It makes blood pressure go up. High blood pressure can be dangerous.

Liver The liver breaks down alcohol. But alcohol is a poison. Alcohol stays in the liver and causes liver damage. This can lead to liver failure and death.

Stomach Alcohol can cause an upset stomach. Regular heavy drinking can cause holes—called *ulcers*—in the stomach.

Small Intestine Alcohol can destroy chemicals that digest food.

▼ Alcohol affects adults in different ways. Some of the effects of alcohol can lead to injury or death.

How is alcohol harmful?

Even a small amount of alcohol can be harmful—especially for young people. Alcohol prevents normal brain and body growth. That's one reason why it is against the law for young people to buy or drink alcohol. A young person will feel the effects of alcohol more quickly than an adult. No amount of alcohol is safe for a young person to drink.

People who drink even small amounts of alcohol are at risk for injuries. Sometimes they fall. They might run into things. Alcohol users who drive can cause crashes that hurt or kill themselves or people around them.

Alcohol can affect the way people act and treat others. People who drink alcohol are more likely to feel angry and cause fights.

Some people drink a lot of alcohol for many years. Over time heavy drinking can hurt almost every part of the body. Alcohol can kill brain cells, making it hard for the user to think clearly or to remember things.

The liver is an organ that is often damaged by alcohol. The liver removes poisons from the blood. It does other jobs as well. Alcohol can scar the liver. Then the liver can't clean the blood. The liver may stop working. This can cause death.

Finally, for some people, drinking alcohol can lead to a disease called **alcoholism** (AL•kuh•haw•lih•zuhm). Alcoholics, or people with alcoholism, can't stop using alcohol. They know alcohol causes problems for them and for people they care about. But they still need to drink it. If they don't, they become nervous and ill.

Myth: Alcoholics wear dirty clothing and drink in alleys.

Fact: Only about 6 out of 100 alcoholics in the United States are like this. Most alcoholics appear to live normal lives.

▼ **People who drink and then drive are responsible for many car crashes.**

LESSON CHECKUP

Check Your Facts

❶ Why is alcohol especially dangerous for young people?

❷ Why is drinking alcohol a safety risk?

❸ CRITICAL THINKING Why might a person who uses alcohol have trouble learning?

❹ List three organs that are affected by alcohol use.

Use Life Skills

❺ MANAGE STRESS Some adults drink alcohol because they don't know other ways to relax. List three healthful things you do to relax.

MAIN IDEA
To stay safe from alcohol and tobacco, avoid places where people use these drugs. Plan ahead by thinking of ways to say *no*.

WHY LEARN THIS? Avoiding alcohol and tobacco is an important skill that will protect your health and safety.

Refusing to Use Alcohol and Tobacco

You may hear people say "Just say *no* to drugs!" Maybe you think it's not always that easy— especially when friends pressure you to smoke or drink. But saying *no* is important. That little word could save your life!

What are some laws about the use of alcohol and tobacco?

It is against the law for young people to buy or receive from others alcohol and tobacco. You must be at least 21 years old to buy alcohol. In most places you must be 18 years old or older to buy tobacco products. It is against the law for anyone your age to buy alcohol or tobacco.

Laws also protect people from the harmful effects of ETS. Most government buildings are smoke-free. Many other places, such as restaurants, have nonsmoking areas.

The government requires warning labels on alcohol and tobacco packaging that tell about the dangers of using these products. The government hopes warnings will help people avoid the dangers of these products.

◄ **You can choose many healthful drinks.**

How can you stay safe from alcohol and tobacco?

Many adults use more alcohol and tobacco than they really want to. Using these drugs has become a habit they can't quit. Understanding why people use these drugs can help you decide never to start using them.

Many people first try alcohol and tobacco when they are young. They think it will make them look grown up, but many adults don't use these drugs. You may be afraid to say *no* if your friends urge you to try them. To stay safe from alcohol and tobacco, stay away from places where people use them. Find friends who don't want to use these products.

Some people use alcohol and tobacco because ads make using alcohol and tobacco products look fun. The truth is that these products are dangerous.

LIFE SKILLS FOCUS

Refuse Bill and his friend, Lyle, find an open bottle of alcohol at Lyle's house. Lyle tells Bill he has heard it is fun to drink alcohol. Lyle wants to try the alcohol. He wants Bill to try it too. How can Bill use what he knows about alcohol to refuse to try it? Use the steps for refusing shown on page *xi*.

• • •

Career

Health Spokesperson

What They Do

Community health spokespersons get information about health-care groups. They tell the public about health information by sending it to newspapers and to TV and radio stations. They also hold events such as health fairs to make people aware of health-care information.

Education and Training

Some community health spokespersons earn college degrees in public relations or health education. Others start as journalists. Some train by getting jobs with public health departments.

skate

How can you say *no* to alcohol and tobacco?

It's important to decide ahead of time that you don't want to use alcohol and tobacco. Then you'll be ready if someone pressures you to try them.

read   sing

Think of some ways you can say *no*. Here are ideas you might try.

- Say *no*, and walk away. You don't have to explain why.
- Make a face. Say, "It doesn't taste good."
- Look surprised. Say, "That's against the law."
- Say, "It's against my family's rules."
- Say, "No, thanks." Then change the subject.
- Laugh and say, "I want to have fun, not hurt my body."
- Look at a clock. Say, "I have to get going."
- Say, "I can have fun without it."
- Say, "I need to be at my best for sports"— or for whatever activities you enjoy.

CONSUMER
FOCUS

Analyze Advertising and Media Messages
Most ads use "tricks" to sell a product. Being able to identify these "tricks" could help you plan ways to refuse alcohol and tobacco. Find an alcohol or tobacco ad. Use page *xv* to figure out a "trick" being used in the ad. Then write a way to refuse the product the ad is trying to sell.

Practice with your family ways to say *no*. Or practice with a friend who has also decided not to use alcohol or tobacco. Try out different ways. Choose the ways you are most comfortable with. When the time comes to say *no*, one of them is sure to feel right. Remember, when you say *no*, you might be saving your health—or your life!

Activity **Say *Yes* to Good Health** When you say *no* to alcohol and tobacco, you can say *yes* to the many activities you enjoy. Without alcohol or nicotine your mind and body work at their best. What activities would you like to say *yes* to? List five things you like to do. Then list ways in which using alcohol or tobacco could affect these activities.

LESSON CHECKUP

Check Your Facts

1. What are two laws about alcohol and tobacco?

2. How can you avoid people who want you to use alcohol and tobacco?

3. CRITICAL THINKING Why is it important to say *no* to alcohol and tobacco?

Use Life Skills

4. REFUSE Think of a time when you refused to do something a friend wanted you to do. How did you say *no*? What did you think about when you said it? How was that situation like saying *no* to alcohol and tobacco?

REFUSE ALCOHOL
and Tobacco

What will you do if someone asks you to use alcohol or tobacco? Practice learning how to say *no*. Then you'll be ready to refuse to use these drugs.

Learn This Skill

Amy is at Pam's house. Pam's big sister smokes cigarettes. Pam thinks it looks cool. She wants Amy to try it with her. How can Amy say *no*?

Say, "It's against the law."

"This is against the law," Amy tells Pam, "and it's bad for us!"

Say, "I don't want to get into trouble or get sick."

"It won't hurt us," says Pam. "We'll be in big trouble if we get caught," Amy says. "We could get really sick."

Suggest something else to do.

"Why don't you come outside with me to skate?" Amy asks.

Walk away.

"Just try one," Pam says.
"I am not going to try cigarettes," Amy says. "I'm going skating."

Practice This Skill

Use these ideas to help you solve the problems.

Ways to Refuse

- Say, "It's against the law."
- Say, "I don't want to get into trouble or get sick."

- Suggest something else to do.
- Walk away.

A. Derrel's friends say that the tobacco some baseball players chew doesn't hurt the lungs. Help Derrel use refusal skills to end this discussion.

B. Cheryl's friends want to go to a park to play. Cheryl knows that people who use drugs hang out there. How could Cheryl say she doesn't want to go?

Review

USE VOCABULARY

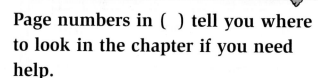

addiction (p. 174)   cancer (p. 175)   nicotine (p. 173)

alcohol (p. 173)   chewing tobacco (p. 174)   smokeless tobacco (p. 174)

alcoholism (p. 181)   environmental tobacco   tar (p. 175)

bloodstream (p. 178)   smoke (p. 176)

Use the terms above to complete the sentences. Page numbers in ( ) tell you where to look in the chapter if you need help.

1. It is hard to quit using tobacco because the nicotine in tobacco causes _____.

2. _____ is a disease in which people "need" alcohol.

3. _____ is a poisonous substance found in all tobacco products.

4. The drug _____ is found in beverages such as beer, wine, and whiskey.

5. The smoke in the air that comes from burning cigarettes is _____.

6. _____ is a dark, sticky substance that coats the lungs of smokers.

7. People who put moist tobacco in their mouths are using _____.

8. Alcohol is carried through the _____ to the brain and the heart.

9. _____ is a dry, powdered form of tobacco that is held between the cheek and gum.

10. A disease that makes cells grow wildly is _____.

CHECK YOUR FACTS

Page numbers in ( ) tell you where to look in the chapter if you need help.

11. Using the diagram, choose three organs that are affected by alcohol and describe the effects. (p. 179)

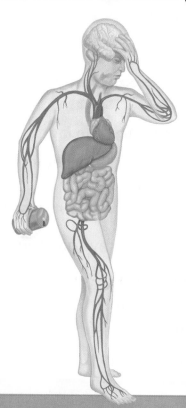

12. How is nicotine harmful to the body? (pp. 173, 175)

13. How does ETS affect nonsmokers? (pp. 176–177)

14. What law about alcohol and tobacco is the most important for young people? (p. 182)

THINK CRITICALLY

15. You hear someone say, "People who don't like alcohol and tobacco shouldn't use them. But they shouldn't try to stop others from using them." Do you agree or not? Explain why.

16. Why do you think advertisers make ads for alcohol and tobacco that show people using these products while having fun?

APPLY LIFE SKILLS

17. **Refuse** A good friend of yours is excited. She has met some older students she really likes. She wants you to go to the mall with her to meet these older students. You go, but as you get near the mall entrance, you see that they are smoking. What would you do?

18. **Communicate** You're at a friend's house after school one day. Your friend's parents aren't home, and your friend says, "Want to try something?" He goes into the refrigerator and takes out a beer. He tells you, "Drink it. It will make you feel great." What would you say?

Promote Health Home and Community

1. Is there a place your family goes to, such as a favorite restaurant, that has environmental tobacco smoke? Discuss ETS with your family. Think of ways your family can avoid ETS there and at other places.

2. A federal law says alcohol can not be sold to anyone under 21 years old. However, states, towns, and counties can have other laws about selling and using alcohol. Make a poster showing local alcohol laws. Display the poster someplace where people in your community can see it.

Activities

Conduct an Interview

At Home • With your family's permission, talk with some people who use tobacco. Ask them how and when they started using tobacco. Ask whether they would like to change the way they use it. Ask them what advice they would offer to someone your age who wants to try tobacco.

Please Don't Smoke

With a Partner • Find out school rules about using alcohol and tobacco. Make a poster for each rule. Display your posters.

Have a Heart

On Your Own • Cut a large heart shape from construction paper. Use it to record all the activities you do in a day. At the end of the day, list the ways your heart helped you. Write what you have learned about decisions you can make that will help keep your heart healthy.

Body Parts Skit

With a Team • Put on a body parts skit. Have people in the skit play different body parts. Each character can explain how alcohol and tobacco affect the body part.

Multiple Choice

Choose the letter of the correct answer.

1. Nicotine is found in _____ products.
   a. tar   b. alcohol
   c. tobacco   d. drug

2. Nonsmokers can get ill by breathing _____.
   a. ETS   b. nicotine
   c. alcohol   d. oxygen

3. Alcohol makes the brain _____.
   a. more alert   b. slow down
   c. speed up   d. bigger

4. Alcoholism is _____.
   a. a disease
   b. a drug
   c. fear of drinking
   d. dislike of alcohol

5. If offered tobacco, _____.
   a. pretend to smoke, but don't
   b. give it a try
   c. impress people with how much you can smoke
   d. say *no* and leave

Modified True or False

Write *true* or *false*. If a sentence is false, replace the underlined term to make the sentence true.

6. Nicotine and alcohol are both <u>drugs</u>.

7. Nicotine causes <u>addiction</u>.

8. ETS affects <u>nonsmokers</u>.

9. Alcohol reaches the heart through the <u>bloodstream</u>.

10. A person's ability to speak and walk are affected by <u>tobacco</u> products.

11. The <u>liver</u> can be scarred by alcohol.

12. <u>A small</u> amount of alcohol is safe for adults to drink.

13. It is harder to <u>keep</u> using alcohol and tobacco than it is to never start at all.

Short Answer

Write a complete sentence to answer each question.

14. What are three tobacco products?

15. What are some health risks caused by smokeless and chewing tobacco?

16. How does alcohol affect the actions of people who drink it?

17. Why can even small amounts of alcohol be harmful to young people?

18. Why is it against the law for people to drive after they drink more than a small amount of alcohol?

Writing in Health

Write paragraphs to answer each item.

19. Explain why using tobacco in ANY form is harmful.

20. Explain why young people who refuse to use drugs are more grown up than those who use them.

CHAPTER 8

Keeping Safe

SAFETY COLLAGE As you read through this chapter, you will learn tips to help keep you safe at home, at school, and at play. Make a collage showing ways to stay safe. You can use photos, draw pictures, or cut out pictures from magazines.

For other activities, visit the Harcourt Learning Site.
www.harcourtschool.com

MAIN IDEA
Following safety rules helps keep you and others safe.

WHY LEARN THIS? What you learn can help protect you and others from harm.

VOCABULARY
- safety rules
- injury
- hazard
- limit
- passenger

Being Responsible for Your Safety

Who is responsible for your safety?

Many people help protect you and keep you safe. At home your family watches over you. Family members have a responsibility, or duty, to protect you.

At school the principal and teachers share the duty of keeping the students safe. Others may also help. The bus driver and the crossing guard help you get safely to school. A hall monitor may help keep the school hallways safe and peaceful. All these people help protect you from harm.

You also have a duty. Your important job is to keep yourself safe. The person most responsible for your safety is **YOU**.

Who is most responsible for your safety? You!

family

bus driver

What does it mean to be careful?

Being careful means that you know and follow safety rules. **Safety rules** are rules that help protect you from injury. An **injury** (INJ•ree) is harm done to a person's body.

One safety rule is to watch out for hazards wherever you are. A **hazard** (HA•zerd) is a danger, like broken glass on a playground, that could lead to an injury. Another safety rule is to obey the limits set by adults. A **limit** (LIH•muht) is a point at which you must stop. Your family probably sets limits by letting you play only in places that are safe.

▼ The pictures show some of the people who help you stay safe. How does each person help protect you? Who is missing? (**Hint**: Who is most responsible for your safety?)

coach

principal

teacher

crossing guard

195

How can you stay safe on the way to and from school?

These safety rules can help keep you safe.

When riding the bus,

- do not bother the driver.

- stay in your seat.

- talk quietly—never yell.

When riding in a car,

- always buckle your safety belt.

- sit in the backseat. It is the safest place for passengers. A **passenger** (PA•suhn•jer) is someone riding in a car or bus with a driver.

When walking,

- stay on the sidewalk.

- walk with others, not alone.

- cross streets only at corners or crosswalks. Before crossing, STOP, LOOK, and LISTEN. THINK about what might be a hazard.

▼ The pictures show ways to keep safe on the road and at school. Which safety rules do you follow?

Talk quietly.

Use safety belts.

How can you stay safe at school?

At school everyone must obey the safety rules. Otherwise, both you and others could get injured.

- Never run in the hallways.
- Don't stand on chairs or other furniture.
- Follow game rules on the playground.
- Don't push or shove.

Sometimes the best safety rule is to get help. Here are two times to get adult help.

- If you see a fight, tell an adult.
- If you see a weapon, such as a gun or a knife, get an adult right away.

JOURNAL

In your Health Journal, write about how you go to and from school. What are the hazards along the way? What safety rules can you follow to make your trip safer?

Use sidewalks.

Walk in school.

LESSON CHECKUP

Check Your Facts

1. Who is most responsible for your safety?
2. Why do you need to watch out for hazards?
3. CRITICAL THINKING What are five safety rules that you follow at school? Name at least two that are not mentioned in this lesson.

Use Life Skills

4. MAKE DECISIONS Imagine that you walk to school with two friends who don't follow safety rules. How could you use the decision-making steps to help them make safer choices? Look on page *ix* if you need help.

MAIN IDEA You can take steps to keep safe around strangers and bullies.

WHY LEARN THIS? What you learn can help protect you from strangers and bullies.

VOCABULARY
• stranger
• trusted adult
• bully

Safety Around Strangers and Bullies

What should you do if you are approached by a stranger?

You need to be very careful around strangers. A **stranger** (STRAYN•jer) is someone you don't know well. You must stay away from people you don't know because some strangers are not safe to be around.

If a stranger approaches, or comes near you, look for a trusted adult to help you. A **trusted adult** is a grown-up you know well or an adult in a responsible position. Usually your family members, teachers, good neighbors, security people, and police officers are adults you can trust.

Strangers in Cars Suppose someone in a car stops next to you and calls to you. What should you do? Follow the rules listed here to be safe.

• Ignore him or her.

• Leave the area. Keep walking, cross the street, or change directions.

• If the stranger gets out of the car or follows you, run away, and yell, "I don't know you!"

Activity **Review Safety Rules** Read this list of safety rules about strangers. What other rules can you add to the list?

Four Safety Rules About Strangers

1. Stay more than an arm's reach away from a stranger.

2. Don't talk to a stranger.

3. Don't take anything from a stranger— not even your own things.

4. Don't go anywhere with a stranger.

Strangers Asking for Help Adults ask other adults, not children, for help. If someone you don't know well asks you for help, here's what to do.

- Tell him or her NO.
- Leave the area.
- Tell a trusted adult.

The Most Important Rule There is one rule that will help you keep safe from strangers. *Always* tell your family where you are going and whom you are with. Don't go *anywhere* with *anyone* unless your family knows about it.

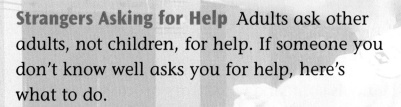

Security Guard

What They Do

Security guards work in banks, amusement parks, museums, and other places where people shop, visit, or live. They help protect people and property. They watch for troublemakers or criminals. They answer questions and help people who are lost or in trouble. Police officers may act as security guards during crowded events such as parades.

Education and Training

Most security guards are high school graduates. They must have good character and have committed no crimes on record. They usually get special training in giving first aid and handling emergencies. They are also trained to stop or capture people who break laws. Some are trained on the job.

This girl cannot find her parents. Why is she asking a security guard for help?

What can you do if someone tries to bully you?

A **bully** is someone who hurts or frightens others, especially those who are smaller or weaker. Here is a story about a bully from one student's journal.

One day a new boy named Justin came to school. He looked mad and did not smile. He was bigger than all the other boys.

The trouble started after school. Justin started calling me names. He pushed me against the wall. I got away. My friends saw it. We told Ms. Díaz, our teacher.

The next day, our class talked about bullies. We drew pictures of what bullies do. We made "No Bullying" posters from our pictures. We acted out ways to get along with others instead of bullying.

It turns out that Justin and I both like to play baseball. We're not really good friends or anything, but he's teaching me how to slide into home plate.

LIFE SKILLS
FOCUS

Communicate
Laura teases Helen because she has freckles and red hair. Helen feels sad when someone teases her. Role-play with a partner to show how Helen could handle how she feels about being teased. Use the steps for communicating shown on page *xii*.

Remember the following safety rules if you have to face a bully.

- Ignore mean remarks. You are not the problem. The bully's problems are causing his or her actions.
- Don't talk back or fight. Walk away.
- Get help if the bully follows you.
- Stay with others. Bullies pick on people who are alone.
- Choose friends who stay away from bullies.

▶ **Finding common interests is one way to get along with a bully.**

LESSON CHECKUP

Check Your Facts

1. What should you do if a stranger approaches you?

2. CRITICAL THINKING Why should you always tell your family where you are going and whom you are with?

3. What should you do if someone tries to bully you?

4. CRITICAL THINKING Describe a situation in which you should ask a trusted adult for help.

Use Life Skills

5. REFUSE Suppose you see an adult stranger looking for a lost dog. The adult asks you to help find the dog. What should you do?

RESOLVE CONFLICTS
Using Negotiation

Conflicts happen, even among friends. Knowing ways to work things out will help you get along better.

Learn This Skill

Pascal, Susan, and Keith want to play table tennis. There are only two paddles. They argue about who gets to play. How can they negotiate, or work together, to resolve their conflict?

1. Agree that you disagree.

"Wait, this isn't getting us anywhere."

2. Listen to each other.

"Let's face it—we can't all play at once. We need a fair way to decide who gets to play."

3. Negotiate.

"We could flip a coin, and the winner will play first."
"We could draw names from a hat."
"We could go in alphabetical order."

4. Compromise on a solution.

"Let's take three pieces of paper and write our names on them. Keith can mix them up, and Pascal will pick two names to play first."

Practice This Skill

Use this summary to help you solve the problems below.

> **Resolve Conflicts**
>
> **1.** Agree that you disagree.
> **2.** Listen to each other.
> **3.** Negotiate.
> **4.** Compromise on a solution.

A. You and a friend decide to play a game. You both want to go first. Use what you know about resolving conflicts to solve this problem.

B. Your friend comes home with you after school. You want to play outside, but your friend would rather play computer games. What do you do?

MAIN IDEA You and your family can take steps to protect yourselves from fire, electricity, and poisons.

WHY LEARN THIS? What you learn can help keep you and your family safe at home.

VOCABULARY
• emergency
• poison

HUMAN BODY CONNECTION

Smoke Alarm
Look at the human respiratory system on pages 12 and 13. Find out where smoke goes in your body if you breathe it in during a fire. Make a list of the organs that are affected by smoke.

Safety at Home—Fire, Electricity, and Poisons

How can you stay safe in a fire?

The smoke alarm beeps. You smell smoke. Someone yells, "Fire!" A house fire is an **emergency** (ih•MER•juhnt•see)—a situation in which help is needed right away. To be prepared, you and your family can work together to make an escape plan and practice fire drills.

Make an Escape Plan Draw a map of your home. Draw arrows to show two ways to escape from each room. Windows or doors may be used. Make sure everyone knows both ways to escape. Choose a place outdoors to meet after you escape. The meeting place could be a tree or a neighbor's house.

Practice Fire Drills Here's how to escape a fire.

- **Crawl out quickly.** If you notice fire or smoke, drop down and stay low. Keep below the smoke so you don't breathe it. As you crawl, hold a damp cloth over your mouth and nose. Breathe through the cloth.

- **Warn others.** Shout or blow a whistle loudly to alert your family.

- **Follow the escape paths.** Crawl along the walls if the smoke is too thick to see through. If you come to a closed door, feel it with your hand. If the door is cool, you may open it.

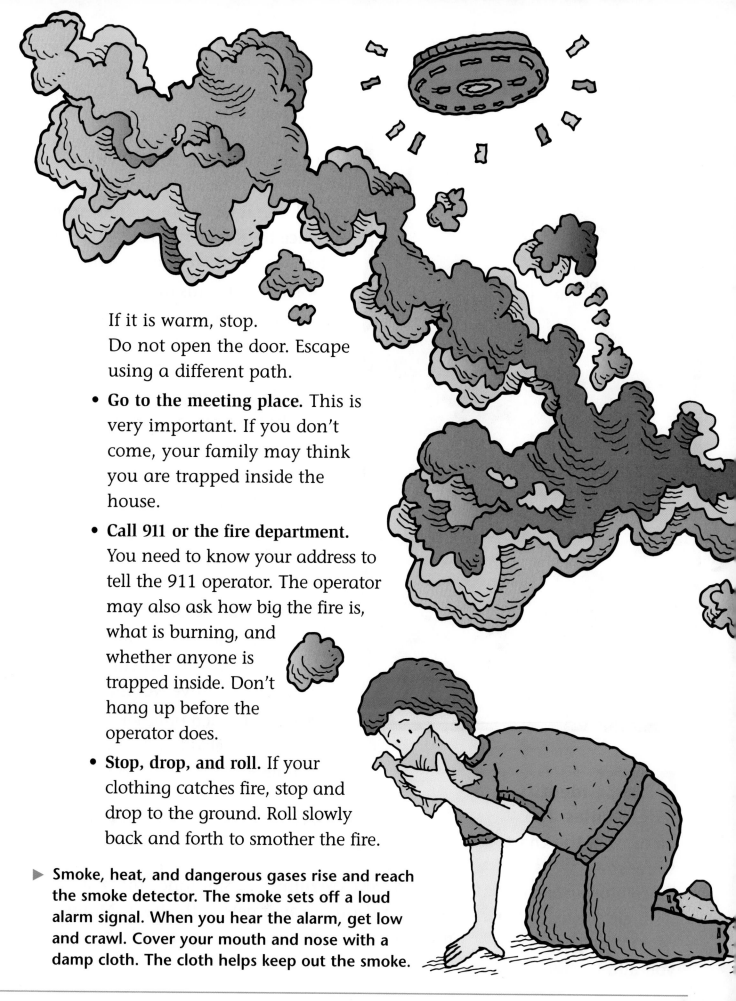

If it is warm, stop. Do not open the door. Escape using a different path.

- **Go to the meeting place.** This is very important. If you don't come, your family may think you are trapped inside the house.

- **Call 911 or the fire department.** You need to know your address to tell the 911 operator. The operator may also ask how big the fire is, what is burning, and whether anyone is trapped inside. Don't hang up before the operator does.

- **Stop, drop, and roll.** If your clothing catches fire, stop and drop to the ground. Roll slowly back and forth to smother the fire.

▶ Smoke, heat, and dangerous gases rise and reach the smoke detector. The smoke sets off a loud alarm signal. When you hear the alarm, get low and crawl. Cover your mouth and nose with a damp cloth. The cloth helps keep out the smoke.

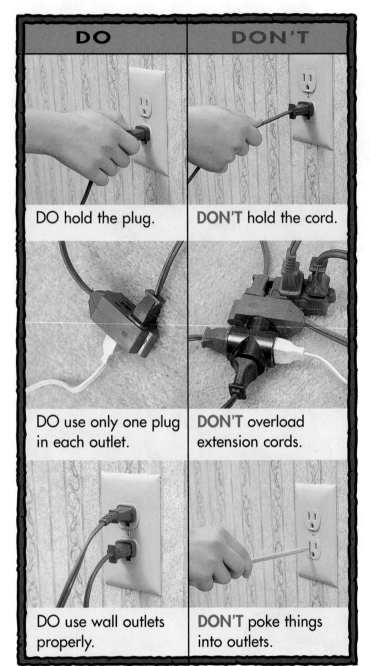

DO	DON'T
DO hold the plug.	**DON'T** hold the cord.
DO use only one plug in each outlet.	**DON'T** overload extension cords.
DO use wall outlets properly.	**DON'T** poke things into outlets.

Activity **Identify Safety Rules** The pictures in the chart show some ways to be safe or unsafe with electricity. What other safety rules can you add?

How can you stay safe around electricity?

Lighting rooms. Drying hair. Keeping food cold. Electricity is very useful. But it also can be dangerous. Practice the safety rules shown and listed here when you use electricity.

- Electrical cords are safe to use only when they aren't cracked or frayed. If you can see the wires inside a cord, don't use it.

- Hold the plug, not the cord, when plugging or unplugging things.

- If there are young children in your home, an adult may want to put covers over the outlets that are not in use.

- Use only one plug in each outlet.

- Never run cords under a carpet.

- To prevent a shock, never plug in or turn on electrical things when you have wet hands.

- NEVER touch outdoor power lines, especially fallen power lines.

How can you stay safe around poisons?

A **poison** (POY•zuhn) is a substance that causes illness or death when it gets in the body. Many useful home products become poisons if they are not used in the right way.

Many products must not be breathed, swallowed, or touched. Even medicines become poisons if too much is taken. These rules will help you stay safe.

- Keep household cleaning products locked up where small children cannot reach them.
- Keep all medicines, even vitamins, locked up and out of the reach of small children.

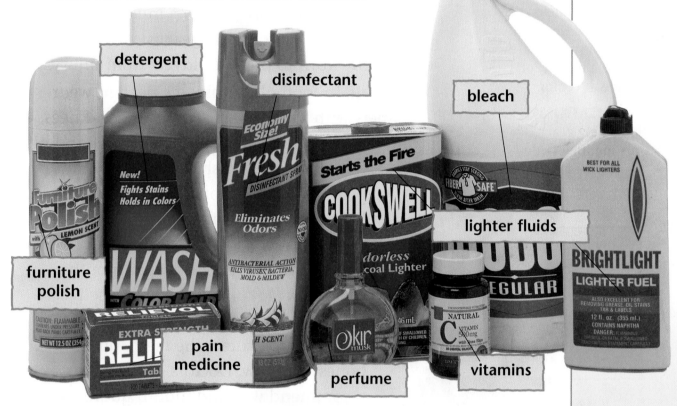

detergent

disinfectant

bleach

furniture polish

lighter fluids

pain medicine

perfume

vitamins

▲ These products can be poisons if not used correctly. Most families keep products like these in their homes. How is each one normally used? Which ones are in your home?

LESSON CHECKUP

Check Your Facts

❶ When a fire breaks out, what information does the 911 operator need?

❷ CRITICAL THINKING Think about the household products in your home. Name four products other than those pictured on this page that could be poisons if used in the wrong way.

❸ List five electricity safety rules.

Set Health Goals

❹ Make a map or floor plan of your home. Draw arrows to show the fire escape paths. Make sure each room has two escape paths such as a door and window. Show where your family members can meet after they escape.

MAIN IDEA
Wearing the proper safety gear helps prevent injuries.

WHY LEARN THIS? What you learn can help keep you safe when you play a sport, skate, ride a bicycle, or ride a scooter.

VOCABULARY
• safety gear
• mouth guard

Safety for Sports and Bicycling

How can you stay safe when playing on a team?

In many team sports, players must wear safety gear in order to play. **Safety gear** is clothing or equipment worn to protect players from injury.

Football In football all players need to wear helmets with face guards. Pads for legs, knees, and shoulders protect players from falls and hits.

Players also wear shoes that have small pegs called cleats on the bottom. Cleats help keep players from slipping on wet grass.

Football players also wear mouth guards. A **mouth guard** is a protective plastic shield worn in the mouth. Mouth guards help protect the teeth, gums, face bones, and jaw. Doctors and dentists recommend wearing mouth guards for most team sports.

Hockey Hockey players are likely to fall or get hit by the sticks or puck. Players wear padding, helmets, and face guards as safety gear. Players also should wear mouth guards.

Softball Softball safety gear includes cleated shoes and padded gloves. However, players are most likely to get injured when batting or running to a base. Batting helmets with ear guards protect batters and runners. A mouth guard also can protect a player.

helmet

shoulder pads

face guard

mouth guard

padded pants

knee pads

cleated shoes

Always wear your safety gear!

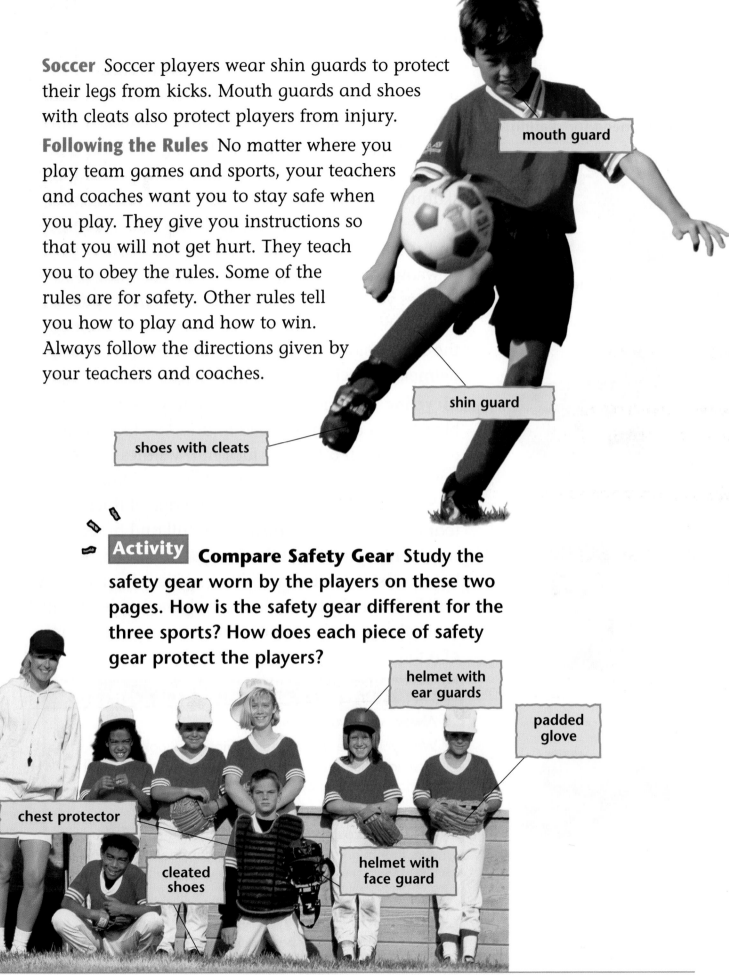

Soccer Soccer players wear shin guards to protect their legs from kicks. Mouth guards and shoes with cleats also protect players from injury.

Following the Rules No matter where you play team games and sports, your teachers and coaches want you to stay safe when you play. They give you instructions so that you will not get hurt. They teach you to obey the rules. Some of the rules are for safety. Other rules tell you how to play and how to win. Always follow the directions given by your teachers and coaches.

mouth guard

shin guard

shoes with cleats

Activity **Compare Safety Gear** Study the safety gear worn by the players on these two pages. How is the safety gear different for the three sports? How does each piece of safety gear protect the players?

helmet with ear guards

padded glove

chest protector

cleated shoes

helmet with face guard

helmet

knee pads

elbow pads

wrist guards

How can you stay safe on wheels?

People playing sports on wheels have high rates of injuries. Skaters, skateboard riders, scooter riders, and bicyclists all need to wear special safety gear.

Skating, Skateboarding, and Riding Scooters The first three pictures on the left show safety gear for skating, skateboarding and riding scooters. Wrist injuries are the most common injuries in skating and skateboarding. Skaters and skateboarders need to wear wrist guards. To avoid elbow and knee injuries you need to wear pads in all three sports.

Skaters and skateboarders also need to protect the fronts, sides, and backs of their heads. Skating helmets protect all sides of the head.

Bicycling The most important safety gear for bicycling is a helmet. Head injuries are likely when a rider falls off a bike. In fact, many states and cities have laws that require bicyclists to wear helmets.

Skate and bicycle helmets are made of thick, hard foam. The foam will crush if you fall and hit your head. This spreads out the force of a fall, so your head doesn't receive all of it. The foam is covered by a slick, hard plastic shell. The slick shell slides when it hits the ground. This takes away some of the force of a fall.

SAFETY RULES FOR BICYCLING

- Always wear your helmet.
- Walk your bike across streets. Stop and look in all directions before you cross. Listen for traffic. Obey all traffic lights and stop signs.
- Carry only one person—YOU!
- Be careful around driveways and parked cars. Watch for cars that might be backing out or car doors that might be opening.
- Ride only in daylight. Use reflective clothes if you must ride in cloudy or rainy weather.
- Avoid wearing heavy backpacks—use a basket.

What should you look for when buying a helmet?

There are many important things to consider when buying a helmet.

- Look for a hard shell and an approval sticker that shows the helmet meets safety standards.

- Buy a bright color to help others see you.

- Wear the helmet level on your head. Make sure it sits evenly between your ears and low on your forehead.

- Make sure the helmet fits. Take the time to fit all the pads and straps. Adjust them so that the helmet is snug but not too tight. Try hard to pull the helmet off. If it comes off, adjust the straps again. If it still comes off, try another helmet.

After buying a helmet, the most important thing to do is to wear it every time you ride. The best helmet in the world won't help you if it's not on your head while you ride.

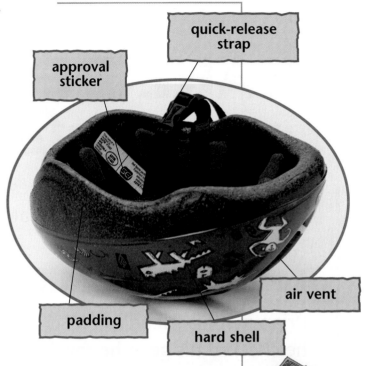

quick-release strap

approval sticker

padding

hard shell

air vent

CONSUMER
FOCUS

Making Buying Decisions
Wearing a helmet for activities such as biking or skating helps keep your head safe from injury. If your helmet doesn't fit anymore, or if you have had an accident with your helmet, you will need to buy a new one. Use the steps on page *xiv* and compare different helmets to decide which helmet is best for you.

LESSON CHECKUP

Check Your Facts

1. Tell what a mouth guard protects and when you should wear one.

2. CRITICAL THINKING How does following the rules of a game help protect the players?

3. What safety gear should be worn while skating and skateboarding?

4. CRITICAL THINKING Why do you think it is important to fit a bicycle helmet properly before buying it?

Set Health Goals

5. List the sports you like to play. Make a chart or drawing that shows the safety gear you need to wear for each sport.

MAKE DECISIONS
with Safety in Mind

Staying safe and avoiding injuries doesn't just happen.
The decisions you make are what keep you safe.

Learn This Skill

Brian met his friends after school to play soccer. When
he checked his gear, he saw he had left his shin guards
at home. How can the steps for making decisions help
Brian make a choice for safety?

1. Find out about the choices you could make.

What are Brian's choices?

2. Imagine the possible result of each choice.

What does Brian think might happen?

3. Make what seems to be the best choice.

"I live only two blocks away. I'll ask my friends to wait for me."

4. Think about what happened as a result of your choice.

Being safe is being smart.

Practice This Skill

Now it's your turn to use your decision-making skills.

Steps for Making Decisions

1. Find out about the choices you could make.

2. Imagine the possible result of each choice.

3. Make what seems to be the best choice.

4. Think about what happened as a result of your choice.

A. You ride your bike to school. When it is time to go home, you can't find your helmet. Decide what to do.

B. An adult you don't know stops his car and offers you a ride. Decide what to do.

MAIN IDEA You can take steps to help when someone gets injured.

WHY LEARN THIS? What you learn can help you treat small injuries and get help in an emergency.

VOCABULARY
• first aid

Getting Help and Giving First Aid

You see a friend trip and fall on the playground. You find your little brother playing with an open bottle of pain killers. Your parent suddenly becomes very ill. What should you do? Get help! At home, tell your family or the baby-sitter. At school, tell a teacher or another adult.

Calling 911 If you can't find an adult, use a telephone to get help. Dial 911 or the emergency number for your area. Tell the operator

• where you are.

• your name and phone number.

• what happened and who needs help.

Calling the Poison Control Center If someone has been poisoned, call the Poison Control Center. Look for the number on the first page of the telephone book, and keep the number handy. Different poisons need different treatments. The people at the Poison Control Center know what to do for each kind of poison.

First Aid No matter how careful you are, you may get small injuries from time to time. Caring for them is called **first aid**. Here are some first-aid tips. Remember, the first thing you should do is tell an adult about the injury, no matter how small. First aid that is properly given can keep a person's injury from getting worse.

First Aid for Cuts and Scrapes

- Wash your hands. Put on gloves to keep the other person's blood off your skin. Blood can carry pathogens.

- Run water over the injury. Rinse away any dirt. Then wash the injury with soap and water.

- Dry the area and put on a clean bandage. Change the bandage every day and when it gets wet or dirty. Keeping the injury clean will help it heal.

First Aid for Insect Bites or Stings

- Find out what kind of insect made the sting or bite.

- Scrape any stinger out. Don't pull it out because more venom may get squeezed into the skin.

- Wash the injury and put ice or a cold pack on it for a few minutes.

LANGUAGE ARTS
CONNECTION

First-Aid Book

With a Team On index cards, write the steps to care for small injuries, such as sunburn, insect bites and stings, blisters, scrapes, cuts, and bruises. Look up any steps you don't know.

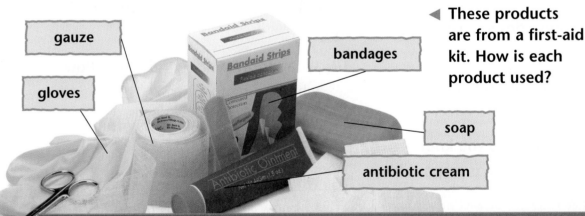

gauze
gloves
bandages
soap
antibiotic cream

◀ These products are from a first-aid kit. How is each product used?

LESSON CHECKUP

Check Your Facts

1. What should you do if someone is badly injured?

2. CRITICAL THINKING If someone has been poisoned, should you give first aid or call the Poison Control Center first? Why?

3. Why is it important not to touch other people's blood?

Set Health Goals

4. Look up the emergency phone numbers on the first page of your local telephone book. Make a card that lists the numbers, such as 911 and the Poison Control Center.

USE VOCABULARY

bully (p. 200)
emergency (p. 204)
first aid (p. 214)
hazard (p. 195)

injury (p. 195)
limit (p. 195)
mouth guard (p. 208)

passenger (p. 196)
poison (p. 206)
safety gear (p. 208)

safety rules (p. 195)
stranger (p. 198)
trusted adult (p. 198)

Use the terms above to complete the sentences. Page numbers in ( ) tell you where to look in the chapter if you need help.

1. An _____ is harm done to the body.

2. A danger that could lead to an injury is called a _____.

3. Rules to keep you from injury are called _____.

4. A _____ is a point at which you must stop.

5. A person who rides in a car or bus with a driver is a _____.

6. A _____ is someone you don't know well.

7. A _____ is a grown-up you know well or someone who is responsible for you.

8. Someone who hurts or frightens others is called a _____.

9. A substance that causes illness or death can be called a _____.

10. Clothing or equipment that can help protect you from injury is _____.

11. A protective shield you wear in your mouth is called a _____.

12. An _____ is a situation in which help is needed right away.

13. The care given to small injuries is _____.

CHECK YOUR FACTS

Page numbers in ( ) tell you where to look in the chapter if you need help.

14. What are two safety rules to follow when riding in a car? (p. 196)

15. Why should you stay away from strangers? (p. 198)

16. What might a 911 operator need to know about a fire emergency? (p. 205)

17. Why do dentists recommend that people wear mouth guards for most team sports? (p. 208)

18. Name four things you need to have in a first-aid kit, and tell how each is used. (p. 215)

19. You are walking to school when a car stops beside you. The driver asks for directions to school. What should you do?

20. Your mom is driving you to school. You want to be safe in the car. Name two things you should do and two things you shouldn't do.

21. **Resolve Conflicts** Jerome and Carlos are on the playground when a bully starts to bother them. How can they negotiate to solve their problem?

22. **Make Decisions** Janine is shopping with her family when she becomes lost. What should she do? Use the steps for making decisions in your answer.

Promote Health - Home and Community -

1. With your family, plan an outdoor hazard hunt. Look for places around your home that could be hazardous. Then discuss ways to correct the hazards.

2. On cards, list emergency numbers for your community. Hand the cards out at school or at a community event.

Activities

A Safer Bicycle

On Your Own • Find out what kind of safety gear bicycles need to have. Then make a poster showing safety gear on bicycles.

Know the Rules

With a Partner • Make a list of different places at your school that you and your classmates use, such as the cafeteria, library, and playground. Make a chart comparing the rules for each of the places you have chosen. List reasons you think some places might need different rules.

First-Aid Kit

With a Team • Visit the school nurse or office and make a list of the first-aid supplies the school has. Make a booklet for a kindergarten class explaining how each item is used.

Safety Search

At Home • Look up *safety* and *fire* in an encyclopedia or in library books. Make a list of fire hazards that are common in homes. Talk about them with your family. Help an adult in your family correct the fire hazards that you find.

Multiple Choice

Choose the letter of the correct answer.

1. The person most responsible for your safety is ____.
   a. your mom   b. your brother
   c. you   d. your teacher

2. Cross a street ____.
   a. at a crosswalk   b. on the left
   c. in the middle   d. on the right

3. If a bully follows you, ____.
   a. turn and talk   b. tell a friend
   c. yell   d. get help

4. If you are trying to escape a fire, ____.
   a. run   b. find water
   c. crawl   d. hide

5. A bicycle helmet should ____.
   a. not have straps   b. fit properly
   c. be black   d. be loose

Modified True or False

Write *true* or *false*. If a sentence is false, replace the underlined term to make the sentence true.

6. Before crossing the street, STOP, LOOK, <u>BLINK</u>, and THINK.

7. The safest place for car passengers to sit is in the <u>front</u> seat.

8. Stay <u>a hand's</u> reach from a stranger.

9. When bullied, <u>stay and fight</u>.

10. One piece of safety gear hockey players wear is a <u>mouth guard</u>.

11. A bicycle helmet should fit <u>loosely</u> on your head.

12. In a fire the cleanest air is <u>up high</u>.

13. Hold the <u>cord</u> when you unplug something.

14. A 911 operator <u>should</u> hang up first.

15. You should put <u>ice</u> on an insect bite.

Short Answer

Write a complete sentence to answer each question.

16. Describe a limit set by an adult.

17. How does a safety belt protect you?

18. Why is safety gear important when you play sports?

19. How could medicine be a poison?

20. Tell what you should do after you escape from a fire.

21. Why shouldn't you plug in a toaster when you have wet hands?

22. Tell why a helmet is important safety gear.

23. What are two safety rules for crossing the street?

Writing in Health

Write paragraphs to answer each item.

24. Give an example of an emergency. Tell what safety steps should be followed in the emergency.

25. What should you look for when you shop for a bicycle helmet?

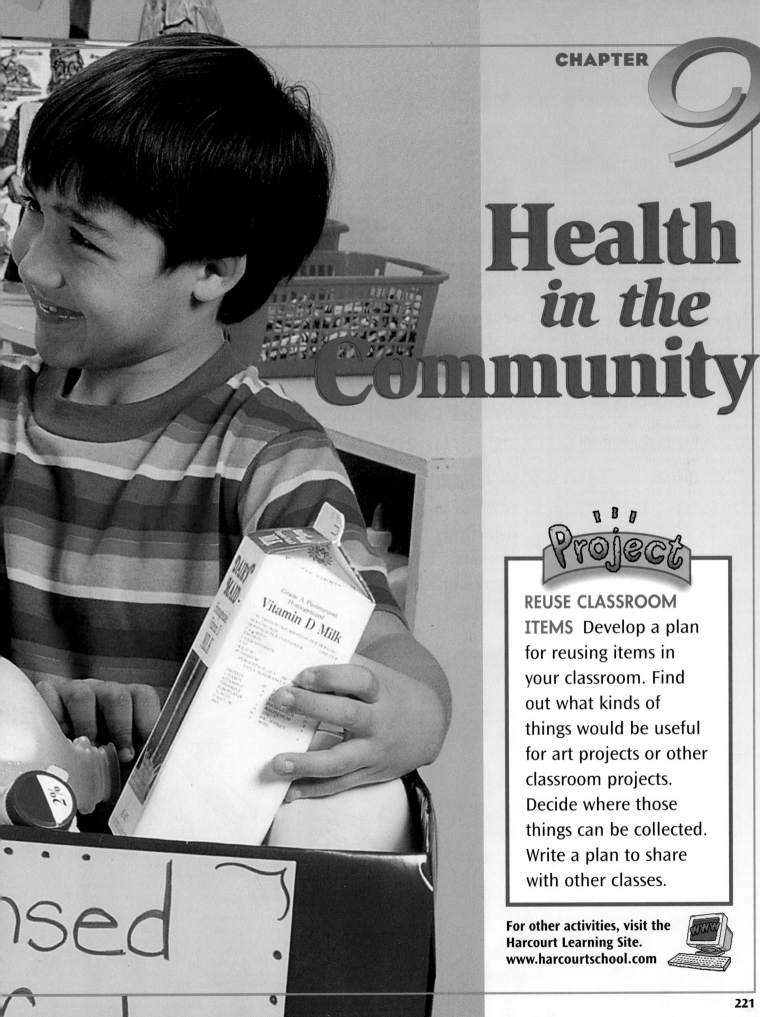

Health
in the
Community

Project

REUSE CLASSROOM ITEMS Develop a plan for reusing items in your classroom. Find out what kinds of things would be useful for art projects or other classroom projects. Decide where those things can be collected. Write a plan to share with other classes.

For other activities, visit the Harcourt Learning Site.
www.harcourtschool.com

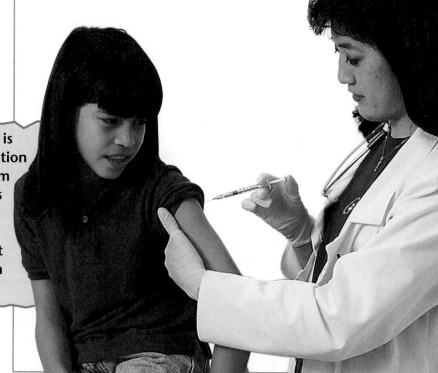

MAIN IDEA
Health departments, hospitals, and clinics treat people who are hurt or ill. They help people stay well, too.

WHY LEARN THIS? You can use what you learn to find places in your community to get health care.

VOCABULARY
- community
- health department
- hospital
- clinic

Health Departments, Hospitals, and Clinics

A **community** (kuh•MYOO•nuh•tee) is a place where people live, work, play, and go to school. Doctors, nurses, and other health care workers help keep the community healthy.

What does a health department do?

A **health department** is a group of health workers that serves a community. Health department workers are also called public health workers. The pictures on pages 222 and 223 show some of the jobs they do.

This public health nurse is giving this girl a vaccination that will protect her from a disease such as mumps or measles. The health department also gives adults shots that protect them from diseases such as flu.

This public health nurse is visiting an older adult in his home. The nurse checks the man's blood pressure. She asks questions to find out if he is well. She checks to see that he is taking the medicine his doctor ordered.

This public health nurse is visiting a new mother at home. The nurse is teaching the mother to care for her baby. Health department workers began helping before the baby was born. They taught the mother which foods to eat and how to take care of herself so that she and the baby would be healthy.

Public health officers keep records of diseases that can spread. They file reports on diseases carried by unsafe food and water. The health department keeps records of animal bites, too. Animals can spread diseases such as rabies.

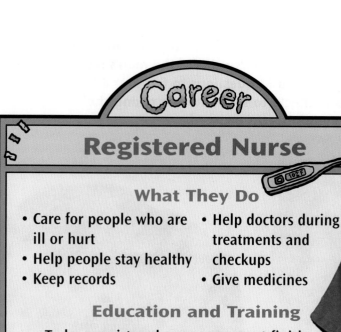

JOURNAL

In your Health Journal, write about a time that you went to a hospital. Perhaps you were visiting a friend or a new baby. If you've never been to a hospital, describe what you think it would be like. Remember, your journal is private and need not be shared with others.

How do hospitals help the community?

A **hospital** (HAHS•pih•tuhl) is a place where hurt or ill people get medical treatment. Hospitals care for people who are too ill to get well at home.

Doctors also take care of people who come to the emergency room. For example, they sew up deep cuts and set broken bones.

Surgeons are doctors who do operations. A surgeon might remove a person's unhealthy appendix. Surgeons also repair organs, such as a person's damaged heart.

Doctors or midwives help women give birth in hospitals. New mothers and their babies get nursing care. Nurses teach mothers how to feed their babies.

How do clinics help the community?

A **clinic** (KLIH•nik) is another place where people go for medical treatment. Sometimes the cost is low or even free. Clinics also teach things such as baby care and car-seat safety.

Doctors and nurses in clinics treat people who are ill or have small injuries. (Very ill or badly hurt people go to the hospital.) Women who are going to have babies often see doctors in clinics.

Clinics offer health screenings—tests to check for diseases. Technicians take blood from patients for tests. Nurses check blood pressure and give eye exams. Nurses also give shots to prevent diseases.

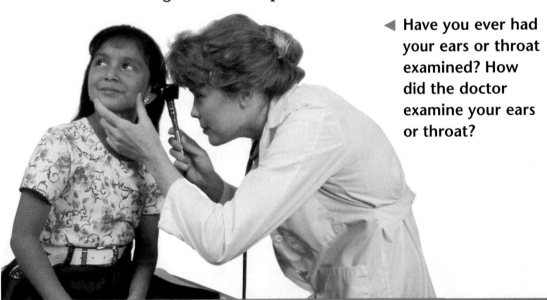

◄ Have you ever had your ears or throat examined? How did the doctor examine your ears or throat?

LESSON CHECKUP

Check Your Facts

❶ Describe three things a health department does.

❷ Name two places in the community where ill or hurt people can get care.

❸ CRITICAL THINKING Why is it important for the health department to keep good records?

❹ Name two services offered at clinics.

Use Life Skills

❺ MANAGE STRESS Write about a health problem that could cause stress. How could a nurse help with this problem?

MAIN IDEA
Clean air and protection from noise are important to your health.

WHY LEARN THIS? You can use what you learn to reduce air and noise pollution and to help keep yourself healthy.

VOCABULARY
• environment
• pollution
• air pollution
• pollution control technician
• noise pollution

▶ The exhaust from cars and trucks has harmful gases and other materials in it. In some areas laws limit the amounts of polluting gases cars and trucks can give off. Drivers in these areas must have their vehicles tested to make sure they meet pollution control laws.

Keeping the Environment Healthful

Everything around you is part of the **environment** (in•VY•ruhn•muhnt). The environment includes all nonliving things, such as rocks and air. It also includes living things, such as trees. You are part of the environment, too.

The environment can be made unhealthful by pollution. **Pollution** (puh•LOO•shuhn) is dirt and harmful materials in the air, water, or land.

How do people keep the air safe?

Dirt and harmful materials in the air are **air pollution**. Some things that people use or do cause air pollution. For example, many people drive to get from one place to another. Cars, trucks, and buses give off materials that pollute the air.

► This pollution control technician tests cars and trucks to see if they meet pollution control laws. He will attach a hose to a vehicle's exhaust pipe. Then he will examine the collected exhaust to see how much harmful material it contains.

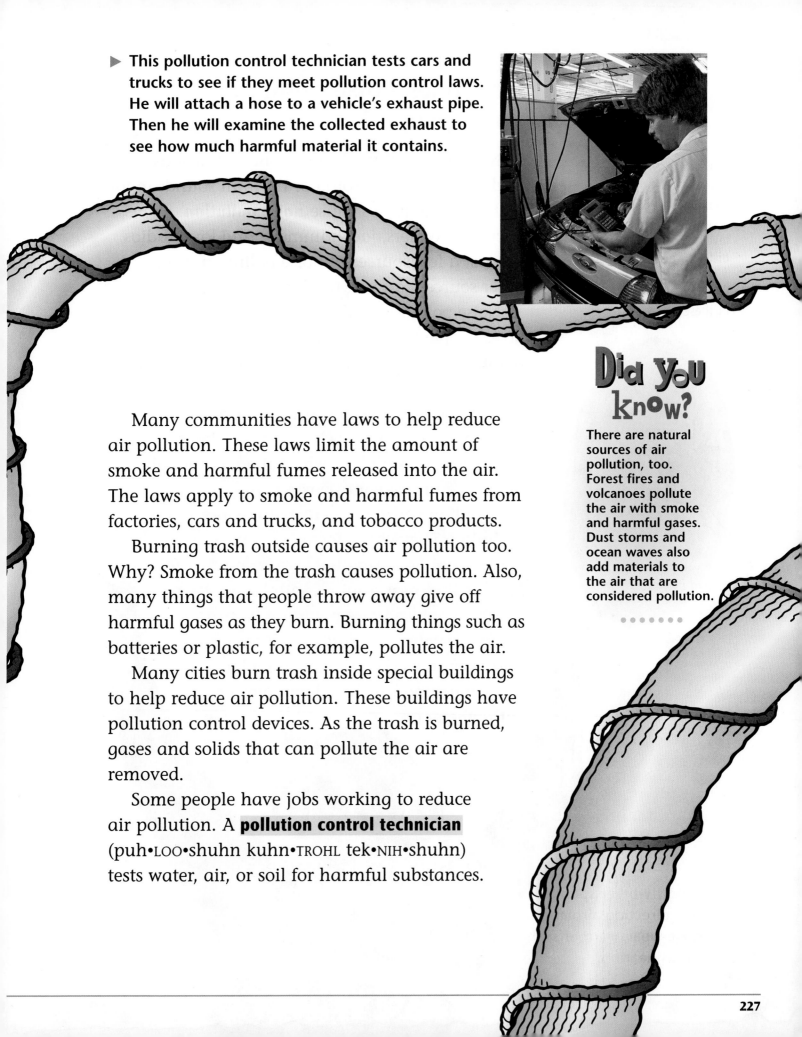

Many communities have laws to help reduce air pollution. These laws limit the amount of smoke and harmful fumes released into the air. The laws apply to smoke and harmful fumes from factories, cars and trucks, and tobacco products.

Burning trash outside causes air pollution too. Why? Smoke from the trash causes pollution. Also, many things that people throw away give off harmful gases as they burn. Burning things such as batteries or plastic, for example, pollutes the air.

Many cities burn trash inside special buildings to help reduce air pollution. These buildings have pollution control devices. As the trash is burned, gases and solids that can pollute the air are removed.

Some people have jobs working to reduce air pollution. A **pollution control technician** (puh•LOO•shuhn kuhn•TROHL tek•NIH•shuhn) tests water, air, or soil for harmful substances.

Did you know?

There are natural sources of air pollution, too. Forest fires and volcanoes pollute the air with smoke and harmful gases. Dust storms and ocean waves also add materials to the air that are considered pollution.

Access Valid Health Information
Noise is measured by how loud it is. Use the steps on page *xvi* to help you research the loudness level of at least five different noises. Make a poster showing ways people can control some of these noises.

• • •

Protect your ears from loud noises.

How does noise pollution affect people?

Noise can pollute the environment, just as dirt in the air can. Disturbing or harmful sounds made by human activities cause **noise pollution**. Sirens, vacuum cleaners, jackhammers, and loud radios are just a few sources of noise pollution. What other sources can you think of?

Noise pollution makes people tired and angry. It gives people headaches and stomachaches. Worst of all, it hurts people's ears. Noise pollution causes most people in the United States to lose some hearing by the time they are 30 years old. If you need to raise your voice for people to hear you, then you are in a place where there is enough noise to damage your hearing.

Pollution control experts help reduce noise pollution. They check factories to make sure workers are not being harmed by unsafe noise levels. Cities make noise control laws. People can help reduce noise pollution by turning down the volume of radios, CD players, and televisions. They can also replace noisy machines, such as lawn mowers, with quieter ones.

▶ **This airport worker spends each day directing airplane traffic. He wears earmuffs to protect his hearing.**

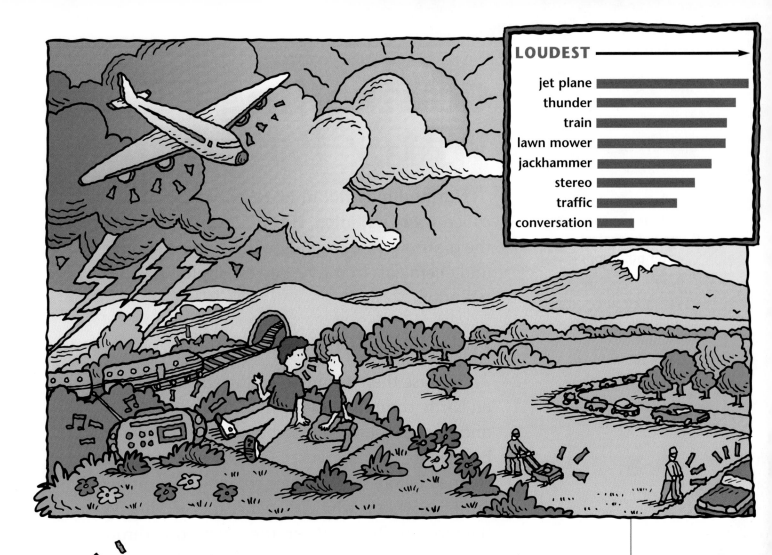

LOUDEST ⟶

- jet plane
- thunder
- train
- lawn mower
- jackhammer
- stereo
- traffic
- conversation

Activity **Compare Noises** This chart shows several sources of noise pollution. List the sounds from softest to loudest. Put a star next to the sounds that are hard to get away from. Put a check mark next to the sounds that can hurt your hearing if they go on for a long time.

LESSON CHECKUP

Check Your Facts

1. Name two kinds of pollution.
2. What does a pollution control technician do?
3. Name two things people can do to help reduce noise pollution.
4. CRITICAL THINKING Name two noises that hurt your ears. How can you protect yourself from those noises?

Set Health Goals

5. Make a list of places you have gone in a car, bus, or truck in the past two days. Make a check mark beside any places you could go safely on foot or on a bike. How does walking or biking when you usually go by car help reduce air pollution?

Controlling Water Pollution

Harmful material in lakes, oceans, or rivers is called **water pollution**. Harmful things poured on the ground can also pollute the water. Garbage and chemicals in a river are examples of water pollution.

How is water kept clean?

Because there is only a certain amount of water on Earth, communities use the same water again and again. The water used to do dishes today will be used for drinking later. Of course, water must be cleaned before it is used for cooking, cleaning, and drinking. That is why dirty water that washes down the drain or flushes down the toilet flows through underground pipes to a sewage treatment plant.

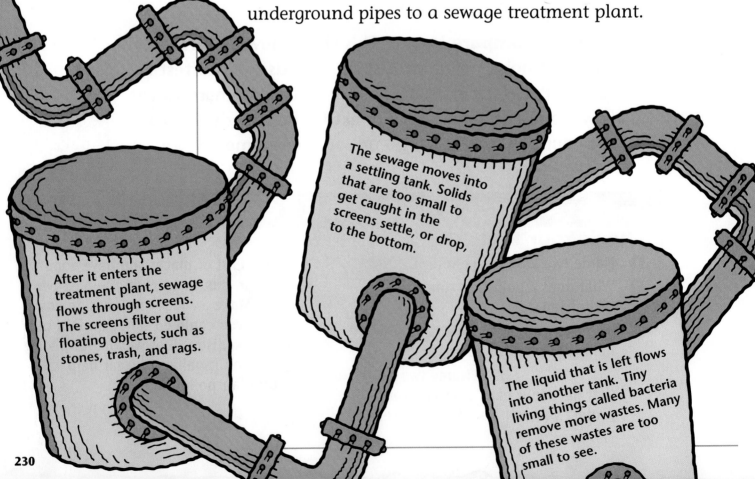

The sewage moves into a settling tank. Solids that are too small to get caught in the screens settle, or drop, to the bottom.

After it enters the treatment plant, sewage flows through screens. The screens filter out floating objects, such as stones, trash, and rags.

The liquid that is left flows into another tank. Tiny living things called bacteria remove more wastes. Many of these wastes are too small to see.

At the sewage treatment plant, the used water, or *sewage*, is treated to make it clean. The pictures on pages 230 and 231 show the main steps in sewage treatment.

The man in the picture is a pollution control technician. He is checking water that has been treated at a sewage treatment plant. He tests it to make sure the water is clean.

Pollution control technicians also check a community's water sources. They take samples from places where communities get their water. They check the samples for pollutants. Some pollutants include used motor oil from cars and trucks and many kinds of chemicals from factories.

If a pollution control technician finds a pollutant, such as oil, in the water, he or she reports it. Then the people or factory that spilled the oil usually pay to clean it up.

Did you know?

One quart (about 1 L) of used motor oil poured onto the ground can pollute 250,000 gallons (about 950,000 L) of groundwater. That's enough water to fill 17 backyard swimming pools.

In another tank, chemicals are added. A chemical called chlorine makes the water clear and kills pathogens.

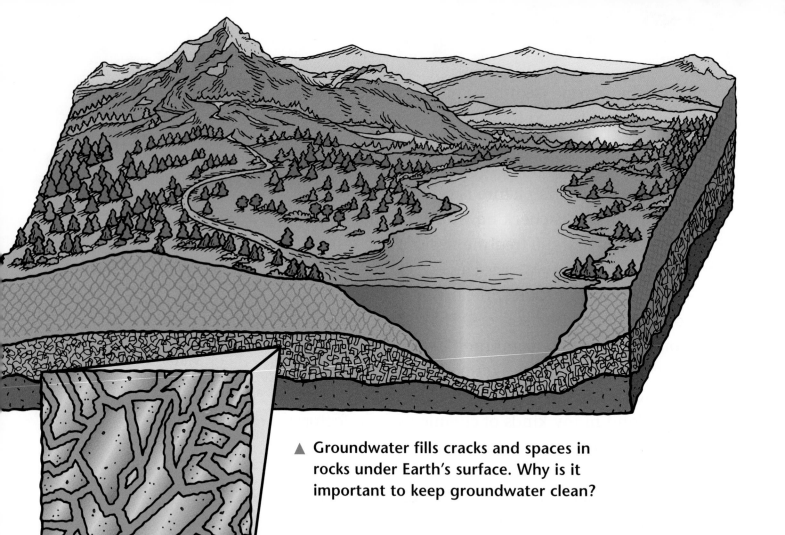

▲ Groundwater fills cracks and spaces in rocks under Earth's surface. Why is it important to keep groundwater clean?

How is groundwater protected?

Many people think we get all our drinking water from lakes and rivers. Yet a lot of drinking water comes from groundwater. **Groundwater** is water that sinks into the soil and fills cracks and spaces in buried rocks. The picture on this page shows an area under Earth's surface where groundwater lies.

Chemicals, such as those used on farms, can travel into the ground and pollute groundwater. Other chemicals, such as those used in factories, can pollute groundwater, too. And salt used on icy highways pollutes groundwater. So can many products that people use to grow grass and to kill garden pests.

LIFE SKILLS FOCUS

Communicate

You and a friend have been painting signs at his house. Your friend wants to pour the leftover paint down the drain. He says it's okay because the water will get treated. What would you say to him? Use the steps for communicating shown on page *xii*.

• • •

These household products can pollute groundwater. If you use them, make sure to get rid of them safely. For example, after you paint a picture, store the paint jar with the lid on tight. Never put leftover paint into the trash or down the drain. Set it aside for a special trash pick-up of toxic, or poisonous, wastes.

Clean water is important to everyone's health. You need clean water for drinking, cooking, bathing, and washing. Talk with friends and classmates about things you can do to help protect groundwater.

LESSON CHECKUP

Check Your Facts

1 What happens to sewage?

2 Where does most drinking water come from?

3 CRITICAL THINKING Would it be a good idea to eat a fish that you caught in a lake that is too polluted to swim in? Explain.

4 CRITICAL THINKING List three ways you can think of to protect rivers where people fish, boat, and swim.

Use Life Skills

5 COMMUNICATE Draw a picture to show a younger student why it is important to keep groundwater clean.

SET GOALS
to Improve Community and Environment

You can do things to improve your community and your environment. Using the steps for setting and reaching goals can help you make a difference in your surroundings.

Learn This Skill

Grant's family went to a lake for a picnic. When they arrived, they saw trash all around. Follow Grant as he uses goal-setting steps to clean up the picnic area.

1. Set a goal.

Grant wanted to make the lake a cleaner place.

2. List steps to reach that goal.

Grant mapped out an area that needed to be cleaned and asked his club friends to help.

3. Monitor progress toward the goal.

4. Evaluate the goal.

Grant and the other members worked together to clean the area around the lake. When each person finished, he or she put an X through his or her section on the map.

After Grant and his friends cleaned up the litter, the entire club enjoyed a picnic at the lake.

Practice This Skill

Use the steps to help you solve the problems below.

> **Steps for Setting Goals**
>
> 1. Set a goal.
> 2. List steps to reach that goal.
> 3. Monitor progress toward the goal.
> 4. Evaluate the goal.

A. Ellen's family recycles aluminum cans. She was upset when she saw all the cans thrown away at school. Use what you know about goal setting to help Ellen.

B. Ray found out that some household products can pollute the groundwater. What goal setting steps could Ray take?

Reduce, Reuse, and Recycle

How can you help the trash problem?

The children in the picture are helping protect the land and water. How? By picking up litter.

Littering (LIH•ter•ing) means dropping trash on the ground or in water. Littering makes beaches, parks, and roadsides ugly. It also harms ocean animals. Many sea turtles die because they eat balloons or plastic bags in the water. They mistake them for jellyfish, their favorite food.

▼ The children cleaning up the beach are wearing heavy gloves. They do this to keep from getting cut by glass or other sharp things found on the beach.

You can help prevent the trash problem by never littering. You might encourage your friends and family members not to litter. You might also pick up litter left by others. If you want to pick up litter in your neighborhood, take a trash bag the next time you take a walk. Spend a few minutes picking up litter at the park or at the beach, too.

Follow two safety rules when you pick up litter. Wear heavy gloves to protect your hands, and get an adult to help you.

The picture below shows many, colorful balloons. The balloons are filled with helium gas, which makes them rise. Never let go of helium balloons. The balloons can travel for many miles and litter the land or the ocean.

LIFE SKILLS FOCUS

Make Decisions

You are outdoors at a friend's house for her birthday party. Her grandfather gives everyone a helium balloon. What should you do with your balloon? Use the steps for making decisions shown on page *ix*.

• • •

◄ If you get a helium balloon, do not let go of it outside. Keep it indoors.

How can you reduce, reuse, and recycle?

Clean land is important to your health. Litter left in uncovered dumps draws flies, mosquitoes, and rats, which may carry disease. We should **reduce**, or make less, trash to stay healthy. For example, you could drink from a glass instead of from a paper cup that would be thrown away.

Another way to reduce trash is to **reuse** something, or use it again. You could reuse outgrown clothes by giving them to someone smaller. You could also reuse books by borrowing them from the library.

Recycling also helps lessen the trash problem. To **recycle** (ree•sy•kuhl) means to collect used things so they can be made into new things.

Some communities recycle newspapers, glass and plastic containers, and cans.

▼ Plastics are stamped with a number code. The numbers 1 through 7 help people at the recycling center sort the plastics. Most (88 percent) of recycled plastics are marked with a 1 or a 2. What products are made from the plastics you recycle?

RECYCLING PLASTICS

Code	Original Objects		New Products
1	Soft-drink bottles, peanut butter jars, precooked frozen-food trays	become...	surfboards, skis, carpets, soft-drink bottles.
2	Detergent bottles, milk and water jugs, margarine cups	become...	flowerpots, trash cans, stadium seats, toys.
3	Shampoo bottles, clear food wrap	become...	floor mats, pipes, hoses, mud flaps on trucks.
4	Grocery bags, bread bags, frozen-food bags	become...	grocery bags, other types of bags.
5	Bottle caps, yogurt cups, other food containers	become...	food trays, car battery parts.
6	Plastic spoons, meat trays, foam cups	become...	trash cans, egg cartons, hangers.
7	Packages with many layers of materials	become...	plastic lumber.

Activity **Learn to Reuse** Look at the things on this page. Tell how each thing was used. Think of at least one new way each thing could be reused. (Hints: You could think about making art. You could also think about gardening.) Tell which of the things are easy to reuse and which are hard to reuse.

LESSON CHECKUP

Check Your Facts

1. Name four ways you can help solve the trash problem.

2. What two safety rules should you follow when you pick up litter?

3. CRITICAL THINKING Which helps prevent the trash problem, buying a cone or a cup of frozen yogurt? Explain.

4. What types of plastic items are commonly recycled? Give at least three examples.

Set Health Goals

5. Write a plan for how you can help solve the trash problem in your classroom. Include in your plan ways you can reduce, reuse, and recycle.

USE VOCABULARY

air pollution (p. 226)

clinic (p. 225)

community (p. 222)

environment (p. 226)

groundwater (p. 232)

health department (p. 222)

hospital (p. 224)

littering (p. 236)

noise pollution (p. 228)

pollution (p. 226)

pollution control technician (p. 227)

recycle (p. 238)

reduce (p. 238)

reuse (p. 238)

water pollution (p. 230)

Use the terms above to complete the sentences. Page numbers in ( ) tell you where to look in the chapter if you need help.

1. Many Americans get their drinking water from ____.

2. A place where people may be able to get health care at a low cost is a ____.

3. Dirt and harmful materials in the air are called ____.

4. When you give a sweater you have outgrown to a younger child, you ____.

5. A place where people live, work, and play is a ____.

6. People who are badly hurt or very sick can get health care at a ____.

7. When you collect glass jars so they can be made into new jars, you ____.

8. Everything around you is part of the ____.

9. If you throw trash on the ground, you are ____.

10. Home health care workers and public health nurses work for the ____.

11. Disturbing or harmful sounds made by human activities cause ____.

12. When you make less trash, you ____.

13. Dirt or harmful materials in the air, water, or land are called ____.

14. Materials that harm lakes, oceans, or rivers are called ____.

15. A worker who tests air, water, or soil for harmful substances is a ____.

CHECK YOUR FACTS

Page numbers in ( ) tell you where to look in the chapter if you need help.

16. Tell three things a health department does. (pp. 222–223)

17. Name three sources of noise pollution. Tell how noise pollution harms health. (p. 228)

18. Describe what happens at a sewage treatment plant. (pp. 230–231)

19. What are some things that can be made from recycled milk jugs? (p. 238)

THINK CRITICALLY

20. If someone has fallen and thinks he might have a broken leg, should he go to the hospital or a clinic? Why?

21. Suppose you buy a loaf of bread at the store. The clerk asks if you want a bag for it. Do you say yes or no? Why?

22. Why do you think it is important for clinics to offer low-cost or free health care?

APPLY LIFE SKILLS

23. **Communicate** Maria's older sister has the radio on very loud. Maria is getting a headache from the loud music. What could Maria say to her sister?

24. **Set Goals** You may have seen your classmates throw away lots of trash every day. Using the goal-setting steps, make a plan to reduce the amount of trash in your classroom.

Promote Health 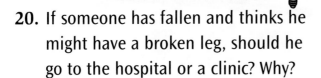 **Home and Community**

1. Cars, trucks, and buses cause air pollution. Talk to your classmates about ways you can help reduce the air pollution problem. For example, could you walk or bike instead of going by car? Make a poster that shows your ideas.
2. With several classmates, think of some new ways your school could recycle. (For example, teachers and staff could use only recycled paper.)

Activities

In the News

On Your Own • Have an adult help you write a letter to your local newspaper. Give ideas for how your community can reduce noise pollution.

Checking Up

With a Partner • Call or visit the health department to find out what children's services they provide. Make a poster to show what you learned.

Save the Groundwater

At Home • Call your trash collection company to find out how your community handles household hazardous wastes such as batteries, paint, and motor oil. Then make a plan for safely getting rid of these harmful wastes in your home.

Payback Time

With a Team • Many states and communities have laws that charge deposits on soft-drink bottles and cans. Then you can return the empty bottles and cans to the grocery store for money. Find out if your state or community has such a law. If so, ask what the grocery does with the bottles and cans. Tell how this can help protect the environment.

Multiple Choice

Choose the letter of the correct answer.

1. Many people in the United States get their drinking water from ____.
   a. oceans   b. groundwater
   c. rivers   d. lakes

2. A place where people live, work, play, and go to school is ____.
   a. a health department
   b. a clinic
   c. a community
   d. a hospital

3. Workers who test water, air, or soil for harmful substances are ____.
   a. pollution control technicians
   b. home health care workers
   c. public health officers
   d. registered nurses

4. A place where a person can get health care is ____.
   a. a hospital
   b. a clinic
   c. a health department
   d. all of these

5. Used water is treated at ____.
   a. a clinic
   b. a hospital
   c. the health department
   d. a sewage treatment plant

Modified True or False

Write *true* or *false*. If a sentence is false, replace the underlined term to make the sentence true.

6. People who are badly hurt can get care at a <u>health department</u>.

7. Harmful materials in the air, water, or land are called <u>pollution</u>.

8. Rocks, air, and trees are all part of the <u>environment</u>.

9. Farm chemicals and salt used on icy roads pollute the <u>air</u>.

10. Giving your clothes to a younger child is an example of <u>reusing</u>.

Short Answer

Write a complete sentence to answer each question.

11. How does burning trash outside harm the environment?

12. Why is it important to keep groundwater clean?

13. What safety rules should you follow when you pick up litter?

Writing in Health

Write paragraphs to answer each item.

14. Tell what happens at a sewage treatment plant.

15. Why do some communities have laws that require car and truck exhaust to be tested for pollutants?

Energy!

Good Nutrition

Preparing Foods Safely

Being Physically Active

Being Safe

First Aid

Alcohol, Tobacco, and Other Drugs

The Food Guide Pyramid

No one food or food group supplies everything your body needs for good health. That's why it's important to eat foods from all the food groups. The Food Guide Pyramid can help you choose healthful foods in the right amounts. By choosing more foods from the groups at the bottom of the pyramid and fewer foods from the group at the top, you will eat the foods that provide your body with energy to grow and develop.

Fats, oils, and sweets
Eat sparingly.

Meat, poultry, fish, dry beans, eggs, and nuts 2–3 servings

Milk, yogurt, and cheese
2–3 servings

Fruit
2–4 servings

Vegetables
3–5 servings

Breads, cereals, rice, and pasta 6–11 servings

Estimating Serving Sizes

Choosing a variety of foods is only half the story. You also need to choose the right amounts. The table below can help you estimate the number of servings you are eating of your favorite foods.

Food Group	Amount of Food in One Serving	Some Easy Ways to Estimate Serving Size
Bread, Cereal, Rice, and Pasta Group	1 ounce ready-to-eat (dry) cereal	large handful of plain cereal or a small handful of cereal with raisins and nuts
	1 slice bread, $\frac{1}{2}$ bagel	
	$\frac{1}{2}$ cup cooked pasta, rice, or cereal	ice cream scoop
Vegetable Group	1 cup of raw, leafy vegetables	about the size of a fist
	$\frac{1}{2}$ cup other vegetables, cooked or raw, chopped	
	$\frac{3}{4}$ cup vegetable juice	
	$\frac{1}{2}$ cup tomato sauce	ice cream scoop
Fruit Group	medium apple, pear, or orange	a baseball
	$\frac{1}{2}$ large banana or one medium banana	
	$\frac{1}{2}$ cup chopped or cooked fruit	
	$\frac{3}{4}$ cup of fruit juice	
Milk, Yogurt, and Cheese Group	$1\frac{1}{2}$ ounces of natural cheese	two dominoes
	2 ounces of processed cheese	$1\frac{1}{2}$ slices of packaged cheese
	1 cup of milk or yogurt	
Meat, Poultry, Fish, Dry Beans, Eggs, and Nuts Group	3 ounces of lean meat, chicken, or fish	about the size of your palm
	2 tablespoons peanut butter	
	$\frac{1}{2}$ cup of cooked dry beans	
Fats, Oils, and Sweets Group	1 teaspoon of margarine or butter	about the size of the tip of your thumb

More Food Guide Pyramids

The Food Guide Pyramid from the U.S. Department of Agriculture (USDA) (page 246) shows common foods from the United States. Foods from different cultures and lifestyles also can make up a healthful diet. These other pyramids can help you add new foods to your diet. Use the serving guide on page 247 with all four pyramids.

Vegetarian

Vegetarians (vej•uh•TEHR•ee•uhns) are people who choose not to eat any meat, poultry, or fish. A balanced vegetarian diet is just as healthful as a balanced diet that includes meats.

Fats, oils, sweets
Eat sparingly.

Dried beans, eggs, nuts, seeds, and meat substitutes
2–3 servings

Milk, yogurt, cheese
2–3 servings

Fruit
2–4 servings

Vegetables
3–5 servings

Bread, cereal, pasta, and rice
6–11 servings

The tops of theses two pyramids differ from the one on page 246. They suggest eating seafood, poultry, eggs and meat each week or month rather than each day. Moderate daily use of vegetable oils is also recommended, What other differences do you notice?

Asian

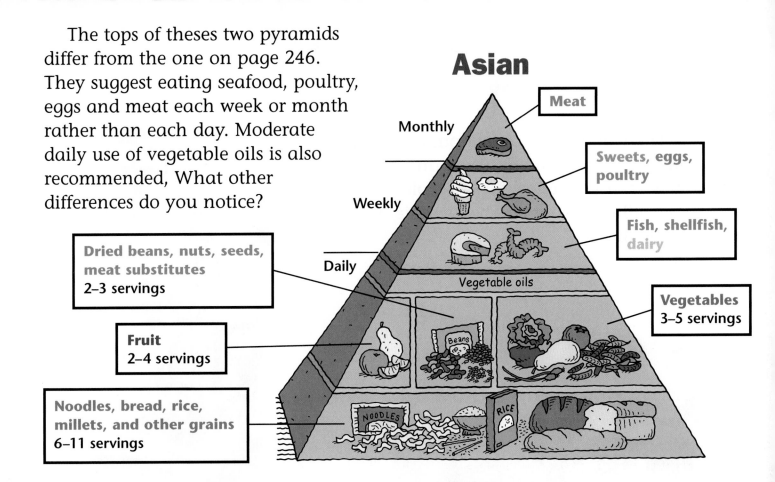

Monthly

Weekly

Daily

Meat

Sweets, eggs, poultry

Fish, shellfish, dairy

Vegetable oils

Vegetables
3–5 servings

Dried beans, nuts, seeds, meat substitutes
2–3 servings

Fruit
2–4 servings

Noodles, bread, rice, millets, and other grains
6–11 servings

Mediterranean

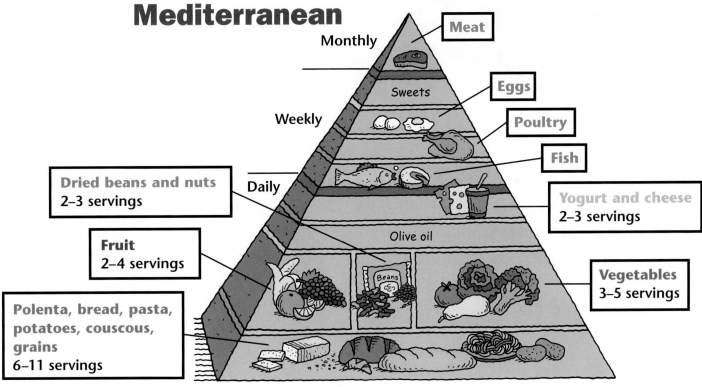

Monthly

Weekly

Daily

Meat

Sweets

Eggs

Poultry

Fish

Yogurt and cheese
2–3 servings

Olive oil

Vegetables
3–5 servings

Dried beans and nuts
2–3 servings

Fruit
2–4 servings

Polenta, bread, pasta, potatoes, couscous, grains
6–11 servings

Dietary Guidelines for Americans

These guidelines come from the USDA. They promote good nutrition and healthful choices. If you follow these simple rules, you will feel better and be healthier your whole life.

Aim for Fitness

- Aim for a healthy weight. Find out your healthy weight range from a health professional. If you need to, set goals to reach a healthier weight.

- Be physically active each day. (Use the Activity Pyramid on page 254 to help you.)

Build a Healthy Base

- Use the Food Guide Pyramid to guide your food choices.

- Each day choose a variety of grains such as wheat, oats, rice, and corn. Choose whole grains when you can.

- Each day choose a variety of fruits and vegetables.

- Keep food safe to eat. (Follow the tips on pages 252–253 for safely preparing and storing food.)

Choose Sensibly

- Choose a diet that is moderate in total fat and low in saturated fat and cholesterol.

- Choose foods and drinks with less sugar. Lower the amount of sugars you eat.

- Choose foods with less salt. When you prepare foods, use less salt.

Fight Bacteria

You probably already know to throw away food that smells bad or looks moldy. But food doesn't have to look or smell bad to make you ill. To keep your food safe and yourself from becoming ill, follow the steps outlined in the picture below. And remember—when in doubt, throw it out!

FIGHT BAC!

Keep Food Safe From Bacteria

CLEAN
Wash hands and surfaces often.

SEPARATE
Don't cross-contaminate.

CHILL
Refrigerate promptly.

COOK
Cook to proper temperatures.

TM

Food Safety Tips

Tips for Preparing Food

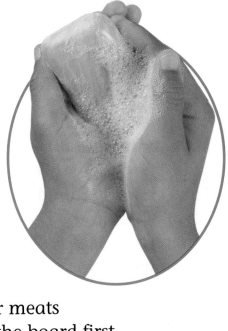

- Wash hands in warm, soapy water before preparing food. It's also a good idea to wash hands after preparing each dish.

- Defrost meat in the microwave or the refrigerator.

- Keep raw meat, poultry, fish, and their juices away from other food.

- Wash cutting boards, knives, and countertops immediately after cutting up meat, poultry, or fish. 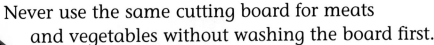Never use the same cutting board for meats and vegetables without washing the board first.

Tips for Cooking Food

- Cook all food completely, especially meat. Complete cooking kills the bacteria that can make you ill.

- Red meats should be cooked to a temperature of 160°F. Poultry should be cooked to 180°F. When done, fish flakes easily with a fork.

- Never eat food that contains raw eggs or raw egg yolks, including cookie dough.

Tips for Cleaning Up the Kitchen

- Wash all dishes, utensils, and countertops with hot, soapy water. Use a soap that kills bacteria, if possible.

- Store leftovers in small containers that will cool quickly in the refrigerator. Don't leave leftovers on the counter to cool.

Planning Your Weekly Activities

Being active every day is important for your overall health. Physical activity helps you manage stress, maintain a healthful weight, and strengthen your body systems. The Activity Pyramid, like the Food Guide Pyramid, can help you choose a variety of activities in the right amounts to keep your body strong and healthy.

The Activity Pyramid

Sitting for more than thirty minutes at a time: Only Once in a While

Light Exercise: Two to Three Times a Week

Flexibility and Strength: Two to Three Times a Week

Twenty-plus minutes of continuous aerobic activity: Three to Five Times a Week

Stay active: Every Day

Guidelines for a Good Workout

There are three things you should do every time you are going to exercise—warm up, work out, and cool down.

Warm-Up: When you warm up, your heart rate, breathing rate, and body temperature increase and more blood flows to your muscles. As your body warms up, you can move more easily. People who warm up are less stiff after exercising, and are less likely to have exercise-related injuries. Your warm-up should include five minutes of stretching, and five minutes of low-level exercise. Some simple stretches are shown on pages 256–257.

Workout: The main part of your exercise routine should be an aerobic exercise that lasts 20 to 30 minutes. Aerobic exercises make your heart, lungs, and circulatory system stronger.

Some common aerobic exercises are shown on pages 258–259. You may want to mix up the types of activities you do. This helps you work different muscles, and provides a better workout over time.

Cool-Down: When you finish your aerobic exercise, you need to give your body time to cool down. Start your cool-down with three to five minutes of low-level activity. End with stretching exercises to prevent soreness and stiffness.

Warm-Up and Cool-Down Stretches

Before you exercise, you should warm up your muscles. The warm-up exercises shown here should be held for at least fifteen to twenty seconds and repeated at least three times. At the end of your workout, spend about two minutes repeating some of these stretches.

▶ **Sit-and-Reach Stretch**
HINT—Remember to bend at the waist. Keep your eyes on your toes!

◀ **Hurdler's Stretch**
HINT—Keep the toes of your extended leg pointed up.

▶ **Upper Back and Shoulder Stretch** HINT—Try to stretch your hand down so that it rests flat against your back.

256

▼ **Thigh Stretch** HINT— Keep both hands flat on the ground. Lean as far forward as you can.

▶ **Calf Stretch** HINT—Keep both feet on the floor during this stretch. Try changing the distance between your feet. Is the stretch better for you when your legs are closer together or farther apart?

▼ **Shoulder and Chest Stretch** HINT—Pulling your hands slowly toward the floor gives a better stretch. Keep your elbows straight, but not locked!

Tips for Stretching

- Never bounce when stretching.

- Hold each stretch for fifteen to twenty seconds.

- Breathe normally. This helps your body get the oxygen it needs.

- Do NOT stretch until it hurts. Stretch only until you feel a slight pull.

Building a Strong Heart and Lungs

Aerobic activities cause deep breathing and a fast heart rate for at least twenty minutes. These activities help both your heart and your lungs. Because your heart is a muscle, it gets stronger with exercise. A strong heart doesn't have to work as hard to pump blood to the rest of your body. Exercise also allows your lungs to hold more air. With a strong heart and lungs, your cells get oxygen faster and your body works more efficiently.

▲ **Swimming** Swimming is great for your endurance and flexibility. Even if you're not a great swimmer, you can use a kickboard and have a great time and a great workout just kicking around the pool. Be sure to swim only when a lifeguard is present.

◄ **In-line Skating** Remember to always wear a helmet when skating. Always wear protective pads on your elbows and knees, and guards on your wrists, too. Learning how to skate, stop, and fall correctly will make you a safer skater.

▼ **Walking** A fast-paced walk is a terrific way to build your endurance. The only equipment you need is supportive shoes. Walking with a friend can make this exercise a lot of fun.

▲ **Jumping Rope** Jumping rope is one of the best ways to increase your endurance. Remember to always jump on an even surface and always wear supportive shoes.

▼ **Bicycling** Bicycling provides good aerobic activity *and* a great way to see the outdoors. Be sure to learn and follow bicycle safety rules. And *always* remember to wear your helmet!

The President's Challenge

The President's Challenge is a physical fitness program designed for students ages 6 to 17. It's made up of five activities that promote physical fitness. Each participant receives an emblem patch and a certificate signed by the President.

The five awards:

 Presidential Physical Fitness Award—presented to students scoring in the top 15 percent in all events.

 National Physical Fitness Award—presented to students scoring in the top 50 percent in all events.

 Health Fitness Award—awarded to all other participants.

 Participant Physical Fitness Award—presented to students who complete all items but score below the top 50 percent in one or more items.

 Active Lifestyle Award—recognizes students who participate in daily physical activity of any type for five days per week, 60 minutes a day, or 11,000 pedometer steps for six weeks.

The Five Activities

1. Curl-Ups or Sit-Ups measure abdominal muscle strength.

- Lie on the floor with your arms across your chest and your legs bent. Have a partner hold your feet.

- Lift your upper body off the ground, then lower it until it just touches the floor.

- Repeat as many times as you can in one minute.

2. **Shuttle Run** measures leg strength and endurance.

- Run to the blocks and pick one up.
- Bring it back to the starting line.
- Repeat for the other block.

3. **One Mile Run or Walk** measures leg muscle strength and heart and lung endurance.

- Run or walk a mile as fast as you can.

4. **Pull-ups** measure the strength and endurance of arm and shoulder muscles.

- Hang by your hands from a bar.
- Pull your body up until your chin is over the bar. Lower your body again without touching the floor.
- Repeat as many times as you can.

5. **V-Sit Reach** measures the flexibility of your legs and back.

- Sit on the floor with your feet behind the line. Your feet should be shoulder-width apart.
- Reach forward as far as you can.

Good Posture at the Computer

Good posture is important when using the computer. To help prevent eyestrain, stress, and injuries, follow the posture tips shown below. Also remember to grasp the mouse lightly and take frequent breaks for stretching.

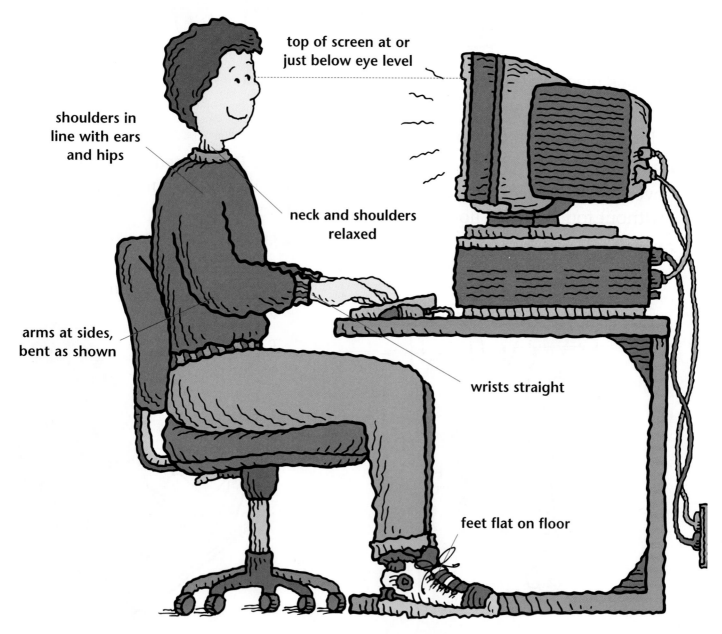

top of screen at or just below eye level

shoulders in line with ears and hips

neck and shoulders relaxed

arms at sides, bent as shown

wrists straight

feet flat on floor

Safety on the Internet

You can use the Internet for fun, education, research, and more. But like anything else, you should use the Internet with caution. Some people compare the Internet to a real city—not all the people there are people you want to meet and not all the places you can go are places you want to be. Just like in a real city, you have to use common sense and follow safety rules to protect yourself. Below are some easy rules to follow to help you stay safe on-line.

Rules for On-line Safety

- Talk with an adult family member to set up rules for going on-line. Decide what time of day you can go on-line, how long you can be on-line, and appropriate places you can visit. Do not access other areas or break the rules you establish.

- Don't give out information like your address, telephone number, your picture, or the name or location of your school.

- If you find any information on-line that makes you uncomfortable, or if you receive a message that is mean or makes you feel uncomfortable, tell an adult family member right away.

- Never agree to meet anyone in person. If you want to get together with someone you meet on-line, check with an adult family member first. If a meeting is approved, arrange to meet in a public place and take an adult with you.

Evaluating Health Websites

Many people find health facts on the Web. However, it's important to remember that almost anyone can put information on the Web. Here are some questions to think about when you are looking at health websites.

Does everyone agree?

Always check the information in more than one source. If several sites agree, the information is probably reliable, or trustworthy.

Who is saying it?

Information from health professionals is usually reliable. Look for the initials of a college degree, such as M.D., R.N., or Ph.D., after the writer's name.

Does the site look good?

Bad design and poor spelling or grammar are signs of a less reliable site.

Are they selling something?

Websites that sell products or services may tell you only what makes their items sound good.

What is the evidence?

Personal stories may sound convincing, but they're not the same as proof. Look for sites that show evidence from science research.

Double-check your facts!

Who controls the website?

Look for sources that you know about. Sites run by universities and the government are usually more reliable (their addresses usually end with .edu or .gov)

Backpack Safety

Carrying a backpack that is too heavy can injure your back. Carrying one incorrectly also can hurt you.

A Safe Weight

A full backpack should weigh between 5 and 10 percent of your body weight. To find 10 percent, divide your body weight by 10. Here are some examples:

Your Weight (lbs)	Maximum Backpack Weight (lbs)
60	6
65	$6\frac{1}{2}$
70	7

▲ This is the right way to wear a backpack.

▲ This is the wrong way to wear a backpack.

Safe Use

• Always use both shoulder straps to carry the pack.

• Use a pack with wide shoulder straps and a padded back.

• Put heavier items in the pack so that they will be closest to your back.

• Store as many books in your locker as you can. Visit your locker often to switch books.

• Avoid carrying a heavy backpack on a bicycle. The weight makes it harder to stay balanced. Use a basket or saddlebags instead.

When Home Alone

Everyone stays home alone sometimes. When you stay home alone, it's important to know how to take care of yourself. Here are some easy rules to follow that will help keep you safe when you are at home by yourself.

Do These Things

- Lock all the doors and windows. Be sure you know how to lock and unlock all the locks.

  - If someone calls who is nasty or mean, hang up. Your parents may not want you to answer the phone at all.

    - If you have an emergency, call 911 or 0 (zero) for the operator. Describe the problem, give your full name, address, and telephone number. Follow all instructions given to you.

    - If you see anyone hanging around outside, tell an adult or call the police.

- If you see or smell smoke, go outside right away. If you live in an apartment, do not take the elevator. Go to a neighbor's home and call 911 or the fire department immediately.

- Entertain yourself. Time will pass more quickly if you are not bored. Try not to spend your time watching television. Instead, work on a hobby, read a book or magazine, do your homework, or clean your room. Before you know it, an adult will be home.

Do NOT Do These Things

- Do NOT use the stove, microwave, or oven unless an adult family member has given you permission, and you are sure about how to use these appliances.

▼ A telephone with a caller ID display can help you decide whether or not to answer the telephone.

- Do NOT open the door for anyone you don't know or for anyone who is not supposed to be in your home.

  - If someone rings the bell and asks to use the telephone, tell the person to go to a phone booth.

  - If someone tries to deliver a package, do NOT open the door. The delivery person will leave the package or come back later.

  - If someone is selling something, do NOT open the door. Just say, "We're not interested," and nothing more.

- Do NOT talk to strangers on the telephone. Do not tell anyone that you are home alone. If the call is for an adult family member, say that they can't come to the phone right now and take a message. Ask for the caller's name and phone number and deliver the message when an adult family member comes home.

- Do NOT have friends over unless you have gotten permission from your parents or other adult family members.

Bike Safety Check

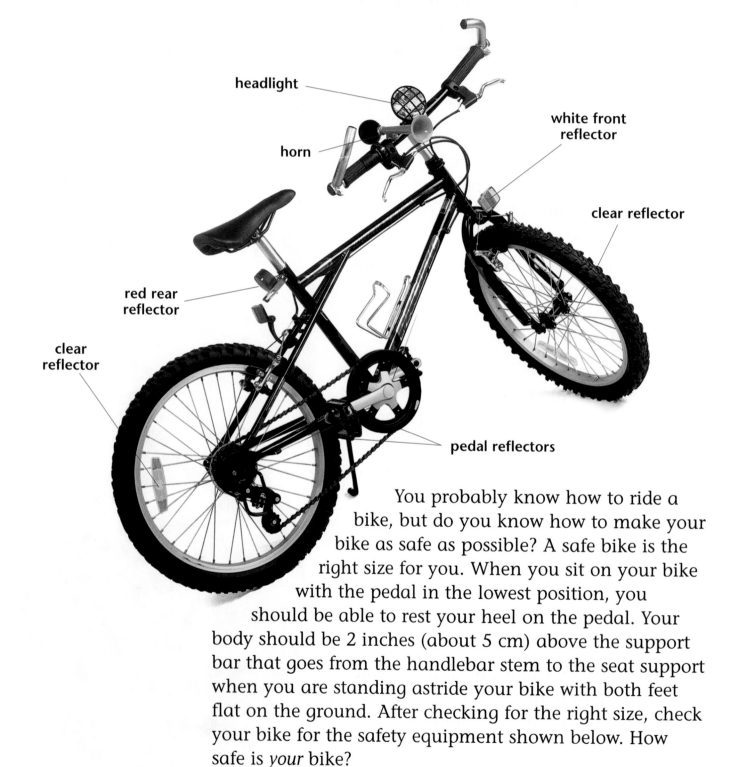

headlight

horn

white front reflector

clear reflector

red rear reflector

clear reflector

pedal reflectors

You probably know how to ride a bike, but do you know how to make your bike as safe as possible? A safe bike is the right size for you. When you sit on your bike with the pedal in the lowest position, you should be able to rest your heel on the pedal. Your body should be 2 inches (about 5 cm) above the support bar that goes from the handlebar stem to the seat support when you are standing astride your bike with both feet flat on the ground. After checking for the right size, check your bike for the safety equipment shown below. How safe is *your* bike?

Your Bike Helmet

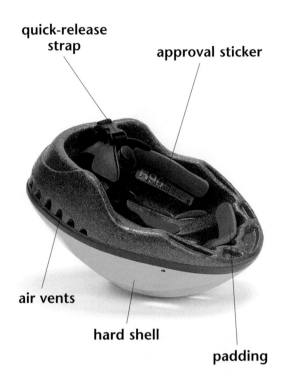

quick-release strap

approval sticker

air vents

hard shell

padding

About 400,000 children are involved in bike-related crashes every year. That's why it's important to *always* wear your bike helmet. Wear your helmet flat on your head. Be sure it is strapped snugly so that the helmet will stay in place if you fall. If you do fall and strike your helmet on the ground, replace it, even if it doesn't look damaged. The hard foam inside the helmet may be crushed, which reduces the ability of the helmet to protect your head in the event of another fall. Look for the features shown here when purchasing a helmet.

Safety While Riding

Here are some tips for safe bicycle riding.

- Check your bike every time you ride it. Is it in safe working condition?

- Ride in single file in the same direction as traffic. Never weave in and out of parked cars.

- Before you enter a street, **STOP**. **Look** left, then right, then left again. **Listen** for any traffic. **Think** before you go.

- Walk your bike across an intersection. **Look** left, then right, then left again. Wait for traffic to pass.

- Obey all traffic signs and signals.

- Do not ride your bike at night without an adult. Be sure to wear light-colored clothing and use reflectors and front and rear lights for night riding.

Safety Near Water

Water can be very dangerous. A person can drown in five minutes or less. The best way to be safer near water is to learn how to swim. You should also follow these rules:

- Never swim without a lifeguard or a responsible adult.

- If you cannot swim, do not use a blow-up raft to go into deep water. Stay in shallow water.

- Know the rules for the beach or pool and obey them. Do not run or shove others while you are near the water.

- Never dive in head-first the first time. Go feet-first instead to learn how deep the water is.

Pool Rules

1. Public use of pool is permitted only when a lifeguard is on duty.
2. All patrons must shower before entering the pool
3. No food, drink, gum, glass, or smoking in the pool or on the deck.
4. No animals in pool or on pool deck
5. Children under 8 years of age must be accompanied by an adult guardian (18 yrs. or older) Children under 6 years of age must be accompained by an adult in the water THIS INCLUDES THE PLAY POOL.
6. In appropriate behavior such as horseplay, fighting, or use of abusive language is not permitted
7. Running is not allowed anywhere in the pool area
8. Diving from the side of the pool in the shallow area is not allowed.
9. Flips or back dives from the side of the pool are not allowed.
10. Only one person at a time is allowed on the diving board. Only one bounce is allowed on the diving board.
11. Only Coast Guard approved flotation devices may be used in the pool.
12. Use of mask, fins, or snorkel is prohibited
13. Loitering or playing in or around the locker rooms, showers, or restrooms is not allowed
14. Only regular, clean bathing suits may be worn Street clothes are not allowed in the pool
15. Bathing load and pool operating hours are posted at the office

► Protect your skin with sunblock and your eyes with sunglasses.

◄ Watch the weather. Get out of the water at once if you see lightning or hear thunder.

▲ Wear a Coast Guard approved life jacket anytime you are in a boat. Wear one when you ride a personal watercraft, too. Know what to do in an emergency.

Fire Safety

1. STOP

Fires cause more deaths than any other type of disaster. But a fire doesn't have to be deadly if you prepare your home and follow some basic safety rules.

- Install smoke detectors outside sleeping areas and on every other floor of your home. Test the detectors once a month and change the batteries twice a year.

- Keep a fire extinguisher on each floor of your home. Check them monthly to make sure they are properly charged.

- Make a family emergency plan. Ideally, there should be two routes out of each room. Sleeping areas are most important, as most fires happen at night. Plan to use stairs only, as elevators can be dangerous in a fire. See pages 274–275 for more about emergency plans.

- Pick a place outside for everyone to meet. Choose one person to go to a neighbor's home to call 911 or the fire department.

- Practice crawling low to avoid smoke.

- If your clothes catch fire, follow the three steps shown here.

2. DROP

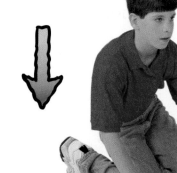

3. ROLL

Storm Safety

- **In a Tornado** Take cover in a sheltered area away from doors and windows. An interior hallway or basement is best. Stay in the shelter until the danger has passed.

- **In a Hurricane** Prepare for high winds by securing objects outside or bringing them indoors. Cover windows and glass with plywood. Listen to weather bulletins for instructions. If asked to evacuate, proceed to emergency shelters.

- **In a Winter Storm or Blizzard** Stock up on food that does not have to be cooked. Dress in thin layers that help trap the body's heat. Pay special attention to the head and neck. If you are caught in a vehicle, turn on the dome light to make the vehicle visible to search crews.

Earthquake Safety

An earthquake is a strong shaking or sliding of the ground. The tips below can help you and your family stay safe in an earthquake.

Before an Earthquake	During an Earthquake	After an Earthquake
• Attach tall, heavy furniture, such as bookcases, to the wall. Store the heaviest items on the lowest shelves. • Check for fire risks. Bolt down gas appliances, and use flexible hosing and connections for both gas and water lines. • Strengthen and anchor overhead light fixtures to help keep them from falling.	• If you are outdoors, stay there and move away from buildings and utility wires. • If you are indoors, take cover under a heavy desk or table, or in a doorway. Stay away from glass doors and windows and from heavy objects that might fall. • If you are in a car, drive to an open area away from buildings and overpasses.	• Keep watching for falling objects as aftershocks shake the area. • Check for hidden structural problems. • Check for broken gas, electric, and water lines. If you smell gas, shut off the gas main. Leave the area. Report the leak.

Make a Family Emergency Plan

By having a plan, your family can protect itself during an emergency. To make an emergency plan, your family needs to gather information, make some choices, and practice parts of the plan.

Know What Could Happen

Learn the possible emergencies in your area, such as fires, storms, earthquakes, or floods. List the possible emergencies.

Have Two Meeting Places

Pick two places to meet. One place should be within a block of your home. The second place should be farther away, for example the main door to your school.

Know Your Family Contact

Choose someone who lives far away to be a contact person. Each family member should memorize the full name, address, and telephone number of the person.

Out-of-State Contact
Ms. Jane Doe
43212 Janeway Blvd.
Big City, IL 12345
(123) 555-1234

Practice Evacuating

During a fire, you need to evacuate, or get out of, your home right away. Use your list of emergencies to plan how to evacuate. Practice evacuating at least twice a year.

▼ This woman is showing her daughter how to turn off the main water valve at their home.

Learn How to Turn Off Utilities

Water, electricity, and gas are *utilities*. Some emergencies may break utilities or make them dangerous. With an adult's help, learn when and how to turn off utilities. **CAUTION:** If you turn off the gas, a professional must turn it back on.

◄ Outdoor water shut-off valve

Make an Emergency Supply Kit

After an emergency, your family may need first-aid supplies or food. Your family can use a checklist from the American Red Cross or another disaster group to make an emergency supply kit.

First Aid

Universal Precautions

You can get some diseases from another person's blood. Universal precautions are steps to protect you from that. Because there is no easy way to tell if someone's blood will make you ill, you should avoid touching anyone's blood. To treat a wound, follow the steps below.

If someone else is bleeding . . .

Wash your hands with soap, if possible.

Put on protective gloves, if available.

Wash small wounds with soap and water. Do *not* wash serious wounds.

Place a clean gauze pad or cloth over the wound. Press firmly for ten minutes. Don't lift the gauze during this time.

If you don't have gloves, have the injured person hold the cloth in place with his or her own hand.

If after ten minutes the bleeding has stopped, bandage the wound. If the bleeding has not stopped, continue pressing on the wound and get help.

If you are bleeding . . .

Follow the steps shown above. You don't need gloves to touch your own blood. Tell an adult about your injury.

For Choking

If someone else is choking . . .

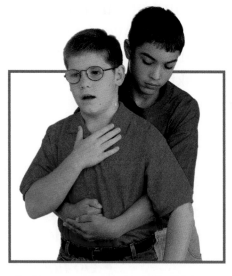

1. Recognize the Universal Choking Sign—grasping the throat with both hands. This sign means a person is choking and needs help.

2. Put your arms around his or her waist. Make a fist and put it above the person's navel. Grab your fist with your other hand.

3. Pull your hands toward yourself and give five quick, hard, upward thrusts on the choker's belly.

If you are choking when alone . . .

1. Make a fist and place it above your navel. Grab your fist with your other hand. Pull your hands up with a quick, hard thrust.

2. Or, keep your hands on your belly, lean your body over the back of a chair or over a counter, and shove your fist in and up.

For Burns

Minor burns are called first degree burns and involve only the top layer of skin. The skin is red and dry and the burn is painful. More serious burns are called second or third degree burns. These burns involve the top layer and lower layer of skin. Second degree burns cause blisters, redness, swelling, and pain. Third degree burns are the most serious. The skin is gray or white and looks burned. All burns need immediate first aid.

Minor Burns

- Run cool water over the burn or soak it in cool water for at least five minutes.
- Cover the burn with a clean, dry bandage.
- Do *not* put lotion or ointment on the burn.

More Serious Burns

- Cover the burn with a cool, wet bandage or cloth.
- Do *not* break any blisters.
- Do *not* put lotion or ointment on the burn.
- Get help from an adult right away.

For Nosebleeds

- Sit down, and tilt your head forward. Pinch your nostrils together for at least ten minutes.
- You can also put an ice pack on the bridge of your nose.
- If your nose continues to bleed, get help from an adult.

For Insect Bites and Stings

- Always tell an adult about bites and stings.

- Scrape out the stinger with your fingernail.

- Wash the area with soap and water.

- Ice cubes will usually take away the pain from insect bites. A paste made from baking soda and water also helps.

- If the bite or sting is more serious and is on the arm or leg, keep the leg or arm dangling down. Apply a cold, wet cloth. Get help immediately!

- If you find a tick on your skin, remove it. Crush it between two rocks. Wash your hands right away.

- If a tick has already bitten you, do not pull it off. Cover it with oil and wait for it to let go, then remove it with tweezers. Wash the area and your hands.

▲ **Deer ticks can carry diseases.**

For Skin Rashes from Plants

Many poisonous plants have three leaves. Remember, "Leaves of three, let them be." If you touch a poisonous plant, wash the area. Put on clean clothes and throw the dirty ones in the washer. If a rash develops, follow these tips.

- Apply calamine lotion or a baking soda and water paste. Try not to scratch. Tell an adult.

- If you get blisters, do *not* pop them. If they burst, keep the area clean and dry. Cover with a bandage.

- If your rash does not go away in two weeks or if the rash is on your face or in your eyes, see your doctor.

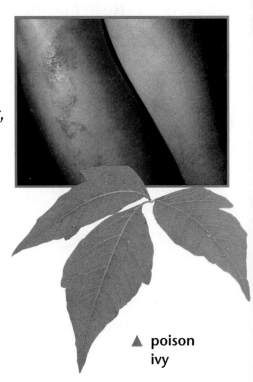

▲ **poison ivy**

What to Do When Others Use Drugs

You should make a personal commitment to not use alcohol, tobacco, or other drugs. But you may be around other students or adults who make unhealthful choices about drugs. Here is what you can do.

Know the Signs

Someone who has a problem with drugs may be sad or angry all the time, skip school or work, or forget events often.

Talk to a Trusted Adult

Do not keep someone's drug use a secret. Ask a trusted adult for help. You can also get support from adults to help you resist pressure to use drugs.

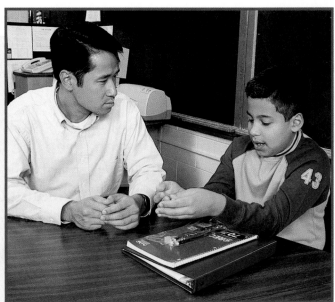

Be Supportive

If a person decides to stop using drugs, help them quit. Suggest healthful activities you can do together. Tell them you are happy that they have quit.

Stay Healthy

Do not stay anywhere that drugs are being used. If you cannot leave, politely ask others not to use drugs while you are there.

Where to Get Help

- Hospitals
- Alateen
- Alcoholics Anonymous
- Narcotics Anonymous
- Al-Anon
- Drug treatment centers

A Drug-Free School

Many schools make rules and sponsor activities to encourage people to say *no* to drugs. This makes the schools a more healthful environment for everyone.

School Rules

Many schools decide to be drug free. They often have strict penalties for anyone found with drugs. For example, a person found with drugs may be expelled or suspended from school.

Positive Peer Pressure

Peer pressure can be bad or good. *Positive peer pressure* is when people the same age encourage each other to make healthful choices. For example, students may make posters or hold rallies to encourage others to choose not to use drugs.

Glossary

Numbers in parentheses indicate the pages
on which the words are defined in context.

PRONUNCIATION RESPELLING KEY

Sound	As in	Phonetic Respelling	Sound	As in	Phonetic Respelling
a	bat	(BAT)	oh	over	(OH•ver)
ah	lock	(LAHK)	oo	pool	(POOL)
air	rare	(RAIR)	ow	out	(OWT)
ar	argue	(AR•gyoo)	oy	foil	(FOYL)
aw	law	(LAW)	s	cell	(SEL)
ay	face	(FAYS)		sit	(SIT)
ch	chapel	(CHAP•uhl)	sh	sheep	(SHEEP)
e	test	(TEST)	th	that	(THAT)
	metric	(MEH•trik)	th	thin	(THIN)
ee	eat	(EET)	u	pull	(PUL)
	feet	(FEET)	uh	medal	(MED•uhl)
	ski	(SKEE)		talent	(TAL•uhnt)
er	paper	(PAY•per)		pencil	(PEN•suhl)
	fern	(FERN)		onion	(UHN•yuhn)
eye	idea	(eye•DEE•uh)		playful	(PLAY•fuhl)
i	bit	(BIT)		dull	(DUHL)
ing	going	(GOH•ing)	y	yes	(YES)
k	card	(KARD)		ripe	(RYP)
	kite	(KYT)	z	bags	(BAGZ)
ngk	bank	(BANGK)	zh	treasure	(TREZH•er)

abdominal muscles (ab•DAH•muh•nuhl MUH•suhlz): body muscles located in the area of the stomach (6)

abstinence (AB•stuh•nuhnts): avoiding a behavior that harms health (139)

addiction (uh•DIK•shuhn): is a constant need that makes people keep using drugs even when they want to stop (174)

aerobic exercises (air•OH•bik EK•ser•sy•zuhz): exercises that strengthen the heart and lungs by making them work harder (82)

air pollution (AIR puh•LOO•shuhn): dirt and harmful materials in the air (226)

alcohol (AL•kuh•hawl): a drug found in beer, wine, and liquor (173)

alcoholism (AL•kuh•haw•lih•zuhm): a disease in which a person can't stop using alcohol (181)

allergy (A•ler•jee): the body's reaction to a substance (132)

anger (ANG•ger): a feeling of being very mad (26)

apologize (uh•PAH•luh•jyz): to say a person is sorry (35)

arteries (AR•tuh•reez): blood vessels that carry blood away from the heart throughout the body (11)

asthma (AZ•muh): a disease that causes people to have difficulty breathing (134)

bacteria (bak•TIR•ee•uh): living things that are so tiny they cannot be seen without a microscope (70, 124)

balanced diet (BA•luhnst DY•uht): a diet in which foods from each food group are eaten each day (105)

biceps (BY•seps): front upper arm muscles (6)

bloodstream (BLUHD•streem): the blood flowing through the body (178)

blood vessels (BLUHD VEH•suhlz): arteries, capillaries, and veins that carry blood throughout the body (11)

body language (BAH•dee LANG•gwij): how the body shows feelings (21)

brain (BRAYN): main organ of the body's nervous systems; control center of body's activities (15)

bully (BU•lee): someone who hurts or frightens others, especially those who are smaller or weaker (200)

caffeine (ka•FEEN): a drug that speeds up the heart (156)

cancer (KAN•ser): a disease that makes cells grow wildly (175)

cavity (KA•vuh•tee): a hole in a tooth (74)

cell (SEL): the smallest working part of the body (58)

chewing tobacco (CHOO•ing tuh•BA•koh): moist tobacco used for chewing (174)

clavicle (KLA•vih•kuhl): collarbone (4)

clinic (KLIH•nik): a place where people get health care (225)

cocaine (koh•KAYN): an illegal drug made from the leaves of the coca plant (161)

communicate (kuh•MYOO•nuh•kayt): to share information (34)

community (kuh•MYOO•nuh•tee): a place where people live, work, play, and go to school (222)

compassion (kuhm•PA•shuhn): the ability to feel what others feel (34)

cool-down (KOOL-down): slow exercise and stretching done for five minutes after hard exercise to help prevent muscle soreness later (89)

deltoid (DEL•toyd): shoulder muscle (6)

dental floss (DEN•tuhl FLAHS): a special thread to remove plaque from between teeth (75)

diabetes (dy•uh•BEE•teez): a noninfectious disease that prevents the body from using sugar properly (135)

diaphragm (dy•uh•FRAM): partition that separates the chest and abdomen (12)

diet (DY•uht): the foods a person usually eats and drinks (99)

disease (dih•ZEEZ): something that causes the body not to work normally (122)

divorce (duh•VORS): when a couple is no longer married to each other (49)

drug (DRUHG): something other than food that changes the way the body works (148)

ear canal (IR kuh•NAL): part of the outer ear where sound enters (2, 78)

eardrum (IR•druhm): located at the end of the ear canal; is moved back and forth by sound waves (2, 79)

emergency (ih•MER•juhnt•see): a situation in which help is needed right away (204)

emotions (ih•MOH•shuhnz): strong feelings (22)

environment (in•VY•ruhn•muhnt): everything, living and nonliving, around you (226)

environmental tobacco smoke (in•vy•ruhn•MEN•tuhl tuh•BA•koh SMOHK): smoke that fills an area when someone is smoking (176)

esophagus (ih•SAH•fuh•guhs): tube made of muscle that squeezes food into stomach (9)

exercise (EK•ser•syz): any activity that makes the body work hard (82)

family (FAM•lee): the group of people with whom a person lives (44)

fear (FIR): the feeling of being scared (24)

feelings (FEE•lingz): the way a person reacts to people and events (18)

femur (FEE•mer): upper leg bone (4)

fever (FEE•ver): a body temperature that is higher than normal (126)

fiber (FY•ber): the woody part of plants; important part of a healthful diet (99)

fibula (FIH•byuh•luh): the outer and smaller of the two bones between the knee and the ankle (4)

first aid (FERST AYD): caring for small injuries (214)

flexors (FLEK•serz): muscles that help bend body parts such as limbs (6)

fluoride (FLAWR•yd): a nutrient the body needs in small amounts that helps keep teeth strong and hard (76, 104)

Food Guide Pyramid (FOOD GYD PIR•uh•mid): a tool to help choose foods for a healthful diet (102)

food label (FOOD LAY•buhl): found on packaged food; gives information about how nutritious a food is (111)

grief (GREEF): a deep sadness (27)

groundwater (GROWND•waw•ter): water that sinks into the soil and fills cracks and spaces buried in rocks (232)

growth rate (GROHTH RAYT): how quickly or slowly a person grows (60)

hazard (HA•zerd): a danger that could lead to an injury (195)

health department (HELTH dih•PART•muhnt): a group of health workers that works for the government and serves the community (222)

heart (HART): organ that pumps blood and keeps it moving through the body at all times (10)

honest (AH•nuhst): truthful (19)

hospital (HAHS•pih•tuhl): a place where hurt or ill people get medical treatment (224)

humerus (HYOO•muh•ruhs): upper arm bone (4)

immune (ih•MYOON): to be protected against a pathogen that causes a disease (129)

infectious disease (in•FEK•shuhs dih•ZEEZ): a disease that can spread from one person to another (124)

ingredients (in•GREE•dee•uhnts): the things that go into a food (110)

inhalants (in•HAY•luhnts): substances that give off fumes (158)

injury (INJ•ree): harm done to a person's body (195)

iris (EYE•ruhs): colored part of the eye that changes size to adjust the amount of light coming into the pupil (2)

large intestine (LARJ in•TES•tuhn): hollow tube in the lower part of the digestive system in which wastes are stored until they leave the body (8)

life cycle (LYF SY•kuhl): four stages of growth people go through (54)

limit (LIH•muht): a point at which a person must stop doing something (195)

littering (LIH•ter•ing): dropping trash on the ground or in water (236)

lungs (LUHNGZ): large, spongy organs used for breathing, located in the chest (12)

marijuana (mair•uh•WAH•nuh): an illegal drug that comes from the hemp plant (160)

medicine (MEH•duh•suhn): a liquid, powder, cream, spray, or pill used to treat illness (130)

mouth (MOWTH): opening through which food passes into the body (8, 12)

mouth guard (MOWTH GARD): a protective plastic shield worn in the mouth (208)

nasal cavity (NAY•zuhl KA•vuh•tee): main opening inside the nose (3)

nerves (NERVZ): bundles of cells that carry messages to and from the brain (14)

nicotine (NIH•kuh•teen): a drug in tobacco (173)

noise pollution (NOYZ puh•LOO•shuhn): disturbing or harmful sounds made by human activities (228)

noninfectious diseases (nahn•in•FEK•shuhs dih•ZEE•zuhz): diseases that are not spread by pathogens and cannot be caught from or spread to other persons (132)

nose (NOHZ): the part of the face between the mouth and eyes that has two openings for breathing and smelling (3)

nostril (NAHS•truhl): opening to the nose (3)

nutrients (NOO•tree•uhnts): the parts of food that help the body grow and get energy (98)

nutrition (nu•TRIH•shuhn): the study of food and how it affects the body (98)

olfactory bulb (ahl•FAK•tuh•ree BUHLB): contains nerves that carry information about odors (3)

olfactory tract (ahl•FAK•tuh•ree TRAKT): part of the nose that carries information from the olfactory bulb to the brain (3)

optic nerve (AHP•tik NERV): part of the eye that transmits nerve signals to the brain (2)

organs (AWR•guhnz): groups of tissues joined together, such as the heart (59)

organ system (AWR•guhn SIS•tuhm): organs that work together (59)

over-the-counter medicine (OH•ver-THUH-KOWN•ter MEH•duh•suhn): a medicine an adult can buy without a doctor's order (150)

passenger (PA•suhn•jer): someone riding in a car or bus with a driver (196)

pathogens (PA•thuh•juhnz): germs that cause disease (115, 124)

peer (PIR): a friend within the same age group (33)

peer pressure (PIR PREH•sher): when friends want someone to do something just because "everyone is doing it" (33)

pelvis (PEL•vuhs): hipbone (4)

plaque (PLAK): a sticky coating that is always forming on teeth (74)

poison (POY•zuhn): a substance that causes illness or death when it gets in the body (206)

pollution (puh•LOO•shuhn): harmful material in the air, water, or land (226)

pollution control technician (puh•LOO•shuhn kuhn•TROHL tek•NIH•shuhn): a person who tests water, air, or soil for harmful substances (227)

pores (POHRZ): tiny holes in the skin (70)

prescription medicine (prih•SKRIP•shuhn MEH•duh•suhn): a medicine that must be ordered by a doctor (151)

private (PRY•vuht): belonging only to a specific person (63)

pupil (PYOO•puhl): hole in center of eye through which light enters the eye (2)

quadriceps (KWAH•druh•seps): front thigh muscles (6)

radius (RAY•dee•uhs): the bone on the thumb side of the forearm (4)

recycle (ree•SY•kuhl): to collect used things so they can be made into new things (238)

reduce (rih•DOOS): to make less of something (238)

refuse (rih•FYOOZ): to say *no* (162)

relationship (rih•LAY•shuhn•ship): the way one person gets along with another person (30)

respect (rih•SPEKT): belief in someone (19)

responsible (rih•SPAHNT•suh•buhl): when a person acts so other people can count on him or her (19)

retina (REH•tuh•nuh): tissue at the back of the eyeball which contains cells that turn images into nerve signals (2)

reuse (ree•YOOZ): to use something again (238)

rib cage (RIB KAYJ): the bones that protect the chest, including the ribs and the bones that connect them (5)

safety gear (SAYF•tee GIR): clothing or equipment worn to protect players from injury (208)

safety rules (SAYF•tee ROOLZ): rules that help protect people from injury (195)

self-control (SELF-kuhn•TROHL): power over emotions (22)

serving (SER•ving): the measured amount of a food probably eaten during a meal or as a snack (102)

sibling (SIH•bling): a brother or sister (49)

side effects (SYD ih•FEKTS): unwanted changes in the body caused by a medicine (155)

skull (SKUHL): the connected bones that protect the brain (4)

small intestine (SMAWL in•TES•tuhn): hollow tube between the stomach and the large intestine through which the body absorbs digested nutrients (8)

smokeless tobacco (SMOHK•les tuh•BA•koh): powdered or shredded tobacco people put between their cheeks and gums (174)

snacks (SNAKS): food between meals (106)

spinal cord (SPY•nuhl KAWRD): bundle of nerves that relays messages between the brain and the rest of the nerves in the body (14)

spine (SPYN): backbone (4)

spoiled (SPOYUHLD): unsafe to eat (114)

stomach (STUH•muhk): organ between the esophagus and the small intestine that squeezes and mashes food (8, 9)

stranger (STRAYN•jer): someone not known well (198)

stress (STRES): a feeling of pressure (25)

sunscreen (SUHN•skreen): a lotion or cream that can protect a person from the sun's harmful rays (73)

symptom (SIMP•tuhm): a sign that something is wrong with the body (122)

tar (TAR): a dark, sticky substance that coats the lungs and air passages of people who breathe in tobacco smoke (175)

taste buds (TAYST BUHDZ): tiny nerve cells on the tongue that pick out tastes and send signals to the brain (3)

tibia (TIH•bee•uh): the inner and larger of the two bones between the knee and the ankle (4)

tissues (TIH•shooz): cells that work together to get a job done (59)

trachea (TRAY•kee•uh): tube that lets air go from the nose and mouth into the chest; also called the windpipe (12)

triceps (TRY•seps): back upper arm muscles (6)

trusted adult (TRUHS•tid uh•DUHLT): a grown-up known well or an adult in a responsible position (198)

ulna (UHL•nuh): the bone on the little-finger side of the forearm (4)

vaccine (vak•SEEN): a substance given to keep someone from getting a certain kind of disease (129)

values (VAL•yooz): strong beliefs, such as honesty and caring about others (44)

veins (VAYNZ): blood vessels that carry blood to the heart (10)

virus (VY•ruhs): a tiny pathogen that causes disease (125)

warm-up (WAWRM-uhp): stretching and slow exercises done for about five minutes that get muscles ready for hard exercise and help prevent pulled muscles (89)

water pollution (waw•ter puh•loo•shuhn): harmful materials in lakes, oceans, or rivers (230)

Index

Boldfaced numbers refer to illustrations.

I-messages,
in communication, 34
in conflict resolution, xiii, 36
Immune, 129
Infectious disease, 124–126
Ingredients, 110–111
Inhalants, 158–159
effects of abuse of, **159**
warning labels, 158
Inhaler, **134**
Injury, 195
treating, 90, **90**
Injury prevention
exercising safely, 88–89
following rules of sport, 209, 210
following safety rules, 195–197
safety gear, 77, 80, 208–211
Inner ear, **2**, **78**
International choking sign, 277
Internet safety, 263
Iris, 2, **2**

Jaw, **5**
Jobs
family responsibilities, 46–47
Jumping rope, 259

Knee pads, **208**

Labels
to help choose healthful foods,
110–111, 137, **157**
to identify dangerous substances,
149
on over-the-counter medicines,
150–151
as warnings, 158, 182
Large intestine, **8**, 99
Laws
about alcohol, 182
against pollution, 227
about tobacco use, 182
Lens, 2, **2**

Lice, head, 127, **127**
Life changes, 54–57
Life cycle, 54–57
Life skills, viii–xvi
communicate, xii, 127, 163, 176,
180, 233
when angry, 26
with family members, 52–53
about feelings, 35, 56, 200
make decisions, ix, 77, 85, 186,
237,
about diet, 102, 105,
108–109
about safe choices, 212–213
manage stress, x
to control disease, 140–141
at school, 28–29
refuse, xi
alcohol, 183
alcohol and tobacco,
186–187
ETS, 139
inhalants, 164–165
unsafe medicines, 154
resolve conflicts, xiii
with family members, 51
with friends, 36–37
using negotiation, 202–203
set goals, viii, 86–87, 234–235
Lifestyle
healthful, 136–139
Listening, 34, 36, 45, 51, 53
Litter, 236–237
Liver,
effects of alcohol on, 179, **179**, 181
Loneliness, 22–23
Loss of loved one. See Grief.
Love, 44
Lung disease
caused by ETS, 177
caused by tobacco, 139, 175
Lungs, 12–13, **12–13**
building strong, 258–259
effects of asthma on, 134
effects of tobacco on, 175

Make decisions. See Life skills.
Making buying decisions xiv, 25, 73,
211
Manage anger, 26
Manage stress. See Life skills.
Marijuana, 149, 160, 161
Measles, 129

Meats,
as food source, 101
on Food Guide Pyramid, 102, **103,
246**
Media messages, analyze advertising
and, xv, 129, 137, 184
Medicine, 130–131, 148, 150–153
alcohol in, 173
consumer safety, 155
forms of, 153
safe use of, 154–155
for treatment of asthma, 134
for treatment of diabetes, 135
in treatment of disease, 130
uses from long ago, 148
Mediterranean food guide pyramid, 249
Middle ear, **2**, **78**
Mouth, **8, 9, 12,** 13
effects of alcohol on, **179**
effects of tobacco on, **175**
protection of, 77, 208–209
Mouth guard, 77, **77**, 208, **208**
Mumps, 129
Muscle pairs, 7, **7**
Muscular system, 6-7, **6–7**
and exercise, 82

Nasal cavity, 3, **3**
Needs, basic, 44
Nerves, 14, **14**
Nervous system, 14-15, **14–15**
cells of, 59, **59**
protection for, 208–210
sense of smell, 3
Nicotine, 173
effects of on brain, 174
Noise pollution, 228–229
Noncommunicable diseases, 132–135
Noninfectious diseases, 132–135
Nonsmokers,
and ETS, 176–177, **176**
Nose, 3, **3**, **12**, 13, 81
Nosebleed, 3, 81, 278
Nostril, **3**
Nutrients, 98, 102, 104, 105, 106, 107
Nutrition, 98, 101
body needs, 98
and diabetes, 135
effects of on circulatory system, 11
effects of on skeletal system, 5
facts, on labels, 111
good health habits, **62**

CREDITS

Cover Design: MKR Design, Inc./Robert B. Allen.

Key: (bkgd) background, (tl) top left, (tc) top center, (tr) top right, (c) center, (bl) bottom left, (bc) bottom center, (br) bottom right.

PHOTOGRAPHS:

Cover: Michael Groen.

Your Health Skills: viii, Ron Kunzman; ix, Ron Kunzman; x, Ron Kunzman; xi, Ron Kunzman; xii, Ron Kunzman; xiii, Ken Kinzie; xiv, Ken Kinzie.

Body Atlas: 1(bl), Eric Camden Photography; (bc), Eric Camden Photography; (br), Digital Imaging Group.

Chapter 1: 16–17(bkgd), Eric Camden Photography; 18–19(c), Todd Champlin; 20(bc), Jeffery Myers/FPG International; 21(tr), Lori Adamski Peek/Tony Stone Images; 22–23(bc), Telegraph Colour Library/FPG International; 24(bl), Digital Imaging Group; 25(tc), Digital Imaging Group; 26(bl), Digital Imaging Group; (bc), Digital Imaging Group; (br), Digital Imaging Group; 27(br), John Henley/The Stock Market; 28(bl), Eric Camden Photography; (br), Eric Camden Photography; 29(tl), Eric Camden Photography; (tr), Eric Camden Photography; 30(bl), John Terence/FPG International; (br), Index Stock; 31(bl), Mark Scott/FPG International; (br), Index Stock; 32(br), J & M Studios/Liaison International; 33(tl), Don Smetzer/Tony Stone Images; 34(bc), Peter Beck/The Stock Market; 35(tl), Arthur Tilley/FPG International; 36(bl), Ed McDonald Photography; (br), Ed McDonald Photography; 37(tl), Ed McDonald Photography; (tr), Ed McDonald Photography; 39(tl), David R. Frazier Photo Library; 40(tr), Stephen Johnson/Tony Stone Images; (bl), Eric Camden Photography.

Chapter 2: 42–43(bkgd), Victoria Bowen Photography; 44(bkgd), Ed McDonald Photography; (bl), Stephen Simpson/FPG International; (bc), Comstock; (br), Comstock; 45(tc), Index Stock; 46(bl), Myrleen Cate/Tony Stone Images; (br), Digital Imaging Group; 47(tc), Comstock; 48(bc), Tom & DeeAnn McCarthy/The Stock Market; 50(bl), Dario Perla/International Stock; 51(tl), Uniphoto; 52(bl), Victoria Bowen Photography; (br), Victoria Bowen Photography; 53(tl), Victoria Bowen Photography; (tr), Victoria Bowen Photography; 54(tl), Index Stock; (tl), Jim Cummins/FPG International; (tc), Comstock; (tr), Earl Kogler/International Stock; (bl), Index Stock; 55(tr), Jim Cummins/FPG International; (br), SuperStock; 56(tr), Comstock; (bl), Earl Kogler/International Stock; 57(tl), Paul Bartony/The Stock Market; (tc), Digital Imaging Group; (tc), Jeff Greenburg/David R. Frazier Photo Library; (tr), SuperStock; 58(bc), Uniphoto; 59(tl), Pete Saloutos/Tony Stone Images; (tc), Dr. Dennis Kunkel/Phototake; (tr), Spike Walker/Tony Stone Images; (c), SuperStock; 60(tl), Ron Chapple/FPG International; (bl), Wright State University/Felf Research Institute; (bc), Wright State University/Felf Research Institute; (br), Wright State University/Felf Research Institute; 61(tl), Richard Gross/The Stock Market; (tl), Elizabeth Hatnon/The Stock Market; (tc), Jade Albert/FPG International; (tc), Jade Albert/FPG International; (tr), Jade Albert/FPG International; (tr), David Young-Wolff/PhotoEdit; 63(br), Ed McDonald Photography; 64(bl), SuperStock; (bc), Dr. Dennis Kunkel/Phototake; (br), Spike Walker/Tony Stone Images; 65(c), Arthur Tilley/FPG International; 66(tc), John Shaw/Tom Stack & Associates; (bl), SuperStock.

Chapter 3: 68–69(bkgd), Victoria Bowen Photography; 70(br), Digital Imaging Group; 72(br), Digital Imaging Group; 74(bl), Digital Imaging Group; 75(tl), Digital Imaging Group; (tr), Digital Imaging Group; 76(bl), Digital Imaging Group; (br), Digital Imaging Group; 77(bl), Digital Imaging Group; (br), Digital Imaging Group; 80(bc), Eric Camden Photography; 81(br), Digital Imaging Group; 82(bl), Eric Camden Photography; 82–83(br), Tony Freeman/PhotoEdit; 83(tr), Eric Camden Photography; (bc), Eric Camden Photography; (br), Bill Wittman; 84–85(bc), Digital Imaging Group; 86(bl), Ed McDonald Photography; (br), Ed McDonald Photography; 87(tl), Ed McDonald Photography; (tr), Ed McDonald Photography; 88(br), Eric Camden Photography; 89(tr), Eric Camden Photography; (bl), Eric Camden Photography; (br), Eric Camden Photography; 90(bl), Ken Kinzie; 91(br), Eric Camden Photography; 94(tr), Tim Davis/Tony Stone Images; (bl), Victoria Bowen Photography.

Chapter 4: 96–97(bkgd), Eric Camden Photography; 98(bl), Vic Bider/Tony Stone Images; (br), Karl Weatherly/Tony Stone Images; 99(tl), Digital Imaging Group; (tr), Digital Imaging Group; 100(tl), Paul Steel/The Stock Market; (tc), Jim Foster/The Stock Market; (tr), Larry Lefever/Grant Heilman Photography; (bc), Joe Sohm/The Stock Market; 101(tl), Michael Rodenfeld/Tony Stone Images; (tr), Michael Newman/PhotoEdit; 103(bkgd), Digital Imaging Group; 104(tl), Digital Imaging Group; (tr), Digital Imaging Group; 105(br), David Madison/Tony Stone Images; 106(bl), Ken Kinzie; 107(br), Digital Imaging Group; 108(br), Eric Camden Photography; 109(tl), Eric Camden Photography; (tr), Eric Camden Photography; 110(bc), Digital Imaging Group; 111(tr), Digital Imaging Group; 114(bc), Digital Imaging Group; 115(bc), Digital Imaging Group; 117(c), SuperStock; 118(bl), Eric Camden Photography.

Chapter 5: 120–121(bkgd), Digital Imaging Group; 122(bc), Ed McDonald Photography; 123(tr), Ed McDonald Photography; 124(bl), Ed McDonald Photography; 125(tl), Jacques Grison/Rapho/Liaison International; (tr), John Michael/International Stock; (br), SuperStock; 126(bl), David Young-Wolff/PhotoEdit; (br), Digital Imaging Group; 127(tl), Ed McDonald Photography; (tr), James Webb/Phototake; 129(tl), Ken Kinzie; 130(bc), Ed McDonald Photography; 131(tr), Ed McDonald Photography; 132(bl), David Young-Wolff/PhotoEdit; 134(bl), Ed McDonald Photography; 135(tr), Ed McDonald Photography; 136(bc), Ed McDonald Photography; 137(tl), Ed McDonald Photography; 138(c), Rudi Von Briel; 139(bl), Ed McDonald Photography; 140(bl), Digital Imaging Group; (br), Digital Imaging Group; 141(tl), Digital Imaging Group; (tr), Digital Imaging Group; 143(tl), Jacques Grison/Rapho/Liaison International; (tl), SuperStock; 144(c), Digital Imaging Group.

Chapter 6: 146–147(bkgd), Digital Imaging Group; 148(br), Digital Imaging Group; 149(tl), Ed McDonald Photography; 150(bc), SuperStock; 151(tc), Rick Brady/Uniphoto; 152(bl), Ed McDonald Photography; (br), Ed McDonald Photography; 153(tl), Ed McDonald Photography; (tr), Paul Barton/The Stock Market; 154(c), Digital Imaging Group; 155(tl), Digital Imaging Group;

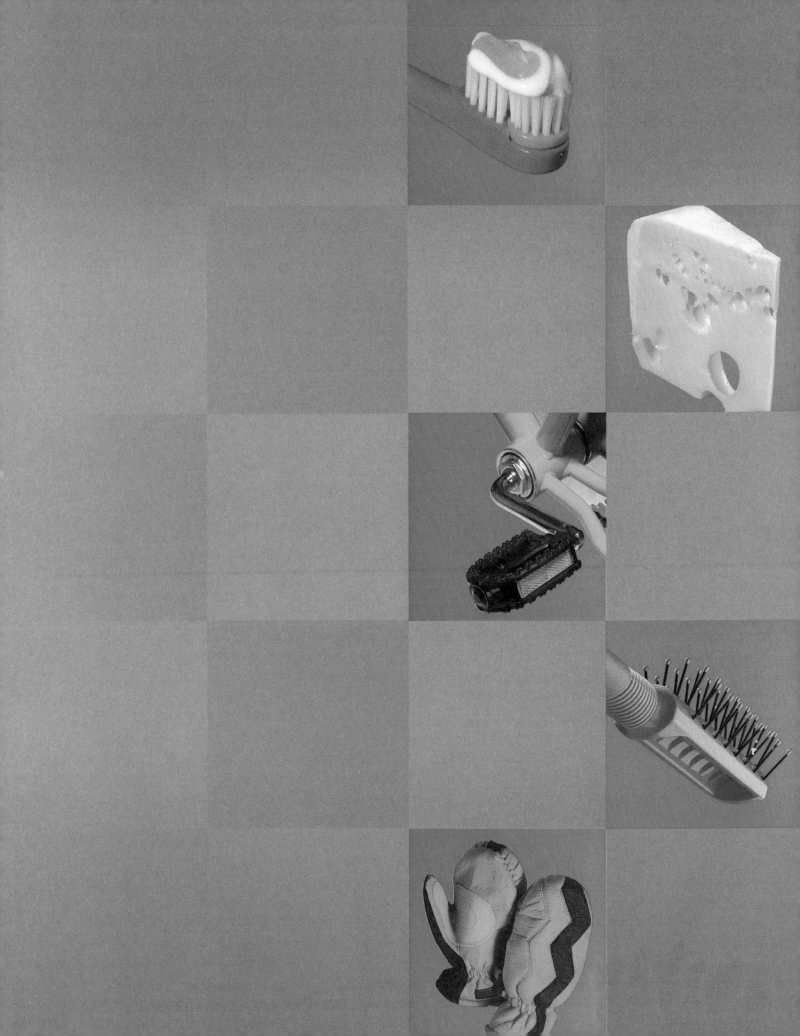

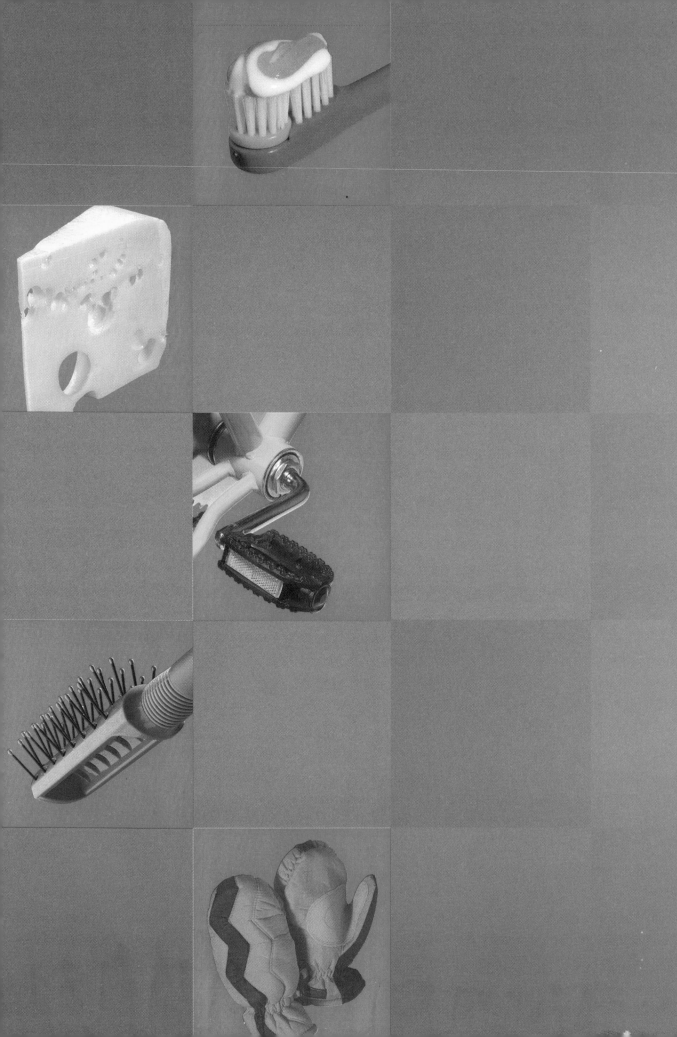